delphi

delphi
by PETER HOYLE

CASSELL · LONDON

CASSELL & COMPANY LTD
35 *Red Lion Square, London WC1*
Melbourne, Sydney, Toronto
Johannesburg, Cape Town, Auckland

© Peter Hoyle 1967
First published 1967

Printed in Great Britain by
The Camelot Press Ltd, London and Southampton
F.267

For Wendy

Preface

SEEN in its peaceful summer beauty, Delphi is a delight to visiting tourists whether they come for a few hours or remain for days in the little village; and the numinous presence of the old gods may yet have power to stir their minds, but, as part of a recommended tour, the sanctuary of Apollo at Delphi does sometimes appear to be another pile of ancient stones, and just one more of the many ruined temples and theatres of Greece. It is because Delphi is different from any other place in Greece, and, for that matter, in the whole world, and is not simply another archaeological site in an exciting setting, that I have written this book. The superb beauty of the site of Delphi is evident, and it was partly because it was so beautiful that it became unique in the past as the spiritual centre of the pan-Hellenic world, and much of what we recognize as the glory of ancient Greece can be attributed to its influence.

Delphi has been loved and revered for so long that there exist innumerable accounts and stories by writers of all periods, and I have drawn freely from their works and fully acknowledge how much I owe to them. Like every one who writes about Greece today, I have had to face the problem of spelling. Where possible I have used the Greek form of names but, particularly in quotation, the Latin version often appears and I must apologize for the inevitable inconsistency.

The influence of Delphi may still be alive today, and there are many people who believe that the ideals of self-knowledge and harmonious relations first expressed there are relevant to our modern world. Wherever I have discussed Delphi I have met with an enthusiastic response, and many organizations and individuals have aided and encouraged me. In particular I must mention Mme Katerina Kakouri, who was not only a friend of Eva and Anghelos Sikelianos and acted with them in the Delphic Festival drama of 1927, but is an authority on the folklore of Greece; Mme Zouzou Nikoloudi, the choreographer of the Arts Theatre of Greece; M. Georges Daux, Director of the French School in Athens, and my Greek teacher, Antonios Georghiades, who first introduced me to the work of modern Greek poets. I am also grateful for the assistance given me by the English School in Athens; the International Theatre Institute of Greece; M. Simon I. Karas, Byzantine musicologist; and not least, the friendly people of Delphi itself.

I should like to acknowledge my gratitude for permission to quote from the following books: Susan Glaspell, *The Road to the Temple* (Ernest Benn, Ltd); P. de la Cost-Messelière, *Delphes* (Les Editions du Chêne); *Callimachus*, translated by A. W. Mair (the Editors of the Loeb Classical Library, Harvard University Press and William Heinemann, Ltd); W. K. C. Guthrie, *The Greeks and Their Gods* (Methuen & Co., Ltd); Edith Hamilton, *The Echo of Greece* (W. W. Norton & Co., Inc.); Charles Seltman, *The Twelve Olympians* (Pan Books, Ltd).

Sophocles, *The Theban Plays*, translated by E. F. Watling; Plato, *The Last Days of Socrates*, translated by Hugh Tredennick; Plato, *The Republic*, translated by D. H. Lee; Lucan, *Pharsalia*, translated by Robert Graves; Thucydides, *The Peloponnesian War*, translated by Rex Warner—all published by Penguin Books, Ltd.

Above all I am grateful to my wife, who not only advised, criticized and worked on the manuscript, but shared the 'enthusiasm', and without whom the book would have hardly been possible.

CONTENTS

ILLUSTRATIONS

1 · *Delphi's Long-deserted Shrine*

DURING the last 150 years the trickle of visitors to Greece has grown into a flood, each visitor inspired in some way with a desire to look at the stones and few remains of what seems to have been a Golden Age when our western culture was first born. There is a legend in the folk-lore of many peoples about a happier time when man was noble and innocent, before the coming of evil, but nowadays, from the pinnacle of our proud achievement in material progress, we do not seriously feel that we are inferior to men of the past. It seems incredible and mysterious that an age which should be past and primitive could produce works of art and reasoned thinking that is in many ways superior to our own. Yet there are doubts in our minds today about our own progress, and a feeling that perhaps we have lost our way. We no longer see so clearly the importance of the relationship between man and the world around him, or the measure of the universe in terms of man himself. Above all things, the ancient Greeks were inspired with a belief in the worth and dignity of man.

> Numberless are the world's wonders, but none
>   more wonderful than man.
> His the might that crosses storm grey seas,
> His are speech and wind swift thought . . .[1]

Sophocles said, in the *Antigone* over 2,000 years ago.

When we find that Classical Greece was no Golden Age but a time when men had human problems and human aspirations, their failures as well as their successes, and a love of life that is no different from our own, their achievements become even more exciting for us to discover.

The triumphs and failures of the Greek spirit found their greatest expression in Delphi, a small place 'far from the sound

[1] Adapted from a translation by Edith Hamilton in *The Echo of Greece*, 1957.

of busy traffic and horses hooves', but one of the most inspiring and dramatic sites in the world.

A hundred miles north-west of Athens at the edge of the Gulf of Corinth lies a long ridge of high, barren mountains, like an impassable rampart which separates the plains of central Greece from the sea, and the trade routes to the west and south. Near the great double peak of Parnassos the little River Pleistos flows into the Gulf of Corinth through a narrow plain of Phokis, which lies between the sea and the mountains. Here in the bay of Itea there is a good landing place and an ancient harbour.

The Pleistos has cut a gorge which penetrates deep into the mountains and makes a breach through which it is possible to climb the rocky walls. The paths lead higher to the pass of Arachova and then descend steeply by winding valleys to the vast flat plain of Boeotia in central Greece. This pass through the mountains has been known and used by men for thousands of years.

On the flank of Parnassos, 2,000 feet up the road from the bay to the pass, there is a natural circus, like an immense theatre, surrounded on three sides by the shoulders of the mountain.[1] Here lies Delphi, suspended in space over the valley of the Pleistos, exposed to the wind and light, one of the most venerated places in the world, and the place which was chosen by the god Apollo, for his domain.

The ancient site lies at the foot of the two vast perpendicular cliffs, which face each other across a deep, echoing gorge. The two precipitous cliffs were well named the Phaedriades, 'the shining ones', as they seem to catch the burning sunlight of summer and intensify it in a focus on Delphi. One of them is now called Rhodini or 'rosy one', because at dawn it shines with early light, the other is Phlemboukos 'the flamboyant' and in the afternoon the sun fires the rock face with an ever-changing glow of colour.

The higher slopes of Parnassos are hidden by these sheer walls of rock whose twin peaks were once thought to be Parnassos itself. From the higher slopes run the underground water courses which rise as springs in and around Delphi, and between

[1] Cf. Strabo. *Geographies*: 9. 3. 3. 'The southern side of Parnassos is occupied by Delphi, a rocky place, theatrelike.'

the walls of the Phaedriades there is a stream that in winter becomes a raging torrent. It foams down the gorge through part of the ancient city of Delphi, down a deep glen, the Pappadia, to join the River Pleistos in the valley far below. There is a terrifying exposure to the forces of nature in Delphi; landslides are frequent and, from earliest times, great rocks have fallen from the heights to damage the buildings below. Apart from the movements of the earth which still shake the houses, the autumn and winter storms are exceptionally violent, and the thunder rolls and echoes backwards and forwards across the mountainside.

To the west of Delphi there is a projecting spur of rock on which the new village is built, on the road to the ancient town of Krissos. From this village the grey-green sea of olive trees can be seen in the plain far below and a view of the distant Gulf of Corinth. Opposite Delphi, across the deep valley of the Pleistos rise the steep cliffs and slopes of Mount Kirphis.

From the foot of the Phaedriades the ground falls away steeply down to the bed of the Pleistos and on this difficult slope a city was once built. The earth is constantly slipping or being washed away by the winter rains, and many artificial terraces had to be made, kept in place by stone walls, both for cultivation as well as for building. About thirty of these terraces rise one above the other supported by ancient masonry, and only the five or six highest are occupied by the true sanctuary of Delphi. The massive retaining walls and foundations even today are threatened by earthquakes and landslides, and continual work of protection and preservation is necessary. It was a measure of the great love and veneration in which Delphi was held that there was so much effort and patience in maintaining a site which was always in danger of destruction by the forces of the mountain, and an indication of the unique part that Delphi played in the history of the Greeks.

It was here, on his first visit to beloved Greece, that the young poet Byron came with his friend Hobhouse, and here, filled with almost unbearable excitement, he saw the great snow-capped mountain of Parnassos and the lonely site of ancient Delphi. For thousands of years in the past and now once again in another age, Delphi on Parnassos was revered as the source of inspiration and the very fount of poetry and music. Byron sat down and wrote the lines which later appeared quite abruptly in his long poem, *Childe Harold*.[1]

> Oh, thou Parnassus! whom I now survey,
> Not in the frenzy of a dreamer's eye,
> Not in the fabled landscape of a lay,
> But soaring snow-clad through thy native sky,
> In the wild pomp of mountain majesty!
> What marvel if I thus essay to sing?
> The humblest of thy pilgrims passing by
> Would gladly woo thine Echoes with his string,
> Though from the heights no more one muse will
>   wave her wing.
>
> Oft have I dreamed of Thee! whose glorious name
> Who knows not, knows not man's divinest love;
> And now I view thee, 'tis alas, with shame
> That I in feeblest accents must adore.
> When I recount the worshippers of yore
> I tremble, and can only bend the knee;
> Nor raise my voice nor vainly dare to soar,
> But gaze beneath thy cloudy canopy
> In silent joy to think at last I look on thee!

In a letter from Greece, Byron wrote: 'Upon Parnassus I saw a flight of twelve eagles, and I seized the Omen. I composed the lines to Parnassus and, on beholding the birds, had a hope that Apollo had accepted my homage.'

The love of Greece, shown by so many people of the western world, is as intense and remarkable today as ever it was during the last two hundred years, as the continually increasing tourist traffic reveals. The long days on the beaches with blue skies and a hot sun that never fails, together with the incomparable charm and hospitality of the Greek people, all combine to make a memorable holiday. But Greece has more to offer than any ordinary Mediterranean holiday resort. However attractive holiday pleasures may be, the most determined sun-bather is drawn to Greece by the knowledge that it is going to be a very special journey of intellectual discovery, and in this he is following in the footsteps of visitors of two thousand years ago, as well as those of more recent times.

The idea of a romantic pilgrimage to Greece started at the end of the eighteenth century when Greece was still under

[1] *Childe Harold*: Canto I: LX-LXI.

Turkish domination. Poets and scholars to whom the history of the fourth century B.C. was often more alive than the affairs of their own times, saw in a journey to Greece the most passionate desire of their lives, and dreamt of the freeing of Greece from foreign rule. Some, like Byron, went to Greece and died in her cause, and others, like the German poet Friedrich Hölderlin, who was obsessed by a love of Greece, never succeeded in visiting her.

A trip to classical lands was part of the liberal education of wealthy scholars but it was often seen as a melancholy journey; a pilgrimage to the sad remains of a distant, glorious, but for ever ended past. Even Byron, after his visit to Delphi, wrote:[1]

> Yet there I've wandered by thy vaunted rill;
> Yes! sigh'd o'er Delphi's long deserted shrine,
> Where, save that feeble fountain, all is still.

Nostalgic sighing over ruins was considered a proper subject for poets of the Romantic period at the beginning of the nineteenth century, and yet no one can visit Greece, and particularly a place like Delphi, and remain unmoved by something more than just the evidence of the past. There comes a time when the past and present seem all one, and something of the awe of the nearness of the old gods comes once again to affect the passing traveller. It is partly due to the landscape, the savage and yet beautiful landscape of mountains with their feet in the blue sea, and islands like jewels, full of sensuous delight, but mostly it is in a quality of the air and light. The intellectual discovery of Greece becomes a journey into brilliance of a very special kind. At midday the luminous air lifts the rocks and islands from the earth and sea until they seem to float in a blaze of light, that was in itself truly holy to the ancient Greeks. At dawn and dusk the colours that paint the landscape are so pure and clear that sky and earth no longer have any definable boundary. The poet who sang of 'Athens with the violet crown'[2] was not using poetic imagery alone. It is perhaps a simple atmospheric effect of the evening light on Mount Hymettus, but its beauty is also a very real blessing from the gods on a lovely city.

[1] *Childe Harold*: Canto I. 1.
[2] Pindar.

The sun-blessed Greeks saw a difference between the dense air breathed by mortals, so often contaminated by the dust and smoke of human activity, and the pure upper atmosphere, the home of the gods, which was called Aether. Aether is the wide expanse of the sky, not just blue or grey but full of light, and the word itself meant 'blazing'. Both the air and aether were literally the breath of life and full of the spirit of god. Although they were two distinct realms, the boundary between them is often hard to define, particularly in Delphi. It was this specially intoxicating mixture that Plutarch, the high priest, wrote about in the second century A.D. 'The air is close and compact, with a tenseness caused by the reflection of the mountains and their resistance, but at the same time fine and biting. It is as fine and close as silk.'[1]

In this clear, luminous atmosphere the gods came very close to earth, bringing their divine inspiration to men. Other civilizations, based on rivers and mud that grew crops, led eventually to material progress, to our industry and engineering, but barren Greece was inspired to become the home of Man's aspirations and the search for the underlying meaning of life itself.

Feeling so near the gods, the ancient Greeks were a deeply religious people and it is impossible to look at a great centre of Greek life and thought like Delphi, without realizing how much the presence of the gods pervaded the everyday lives of the people. The light that is so abundant in Greece was loved in a very special way as an aspect of the god Apollo, and Delphi was the home of Apollo. He was not the greatest of the gods they worshipped, but was greatly revered. It was once the tradition to blow a kiss to him on rising and seeing the first light of day. Of all the gods, he was the most generous and understanding, the far-seeing one whose purpose it was to guide men into the light of reason. At a time when there was the greatest advance in civilization in the history of man, Athene—the goddess of wisdom—with Apollo, became the guardians of Greece. Robert Payne in his *Splendour of Greece* says: 'They were the youngest and sweetest of the gods who ever ruled, lovers of life and the minds soaring flight. They were the harbingers of human freedom against the weight of oppressive tradition.

[1] Plutarch. *Moralia*. Translated by C. W. King, 1903.

They were the new buds bursting forth in a world rotting with corruption.'[1]

Religion in the Greek world was tolerant, there was no religious persecution, and so side by side with ancient superstitions and strange rites, there developed at the finest period of Greek history, a noble and highly sophisticated concept of divinity. In later years it was the best of this Greek thought which so profoundly influenced early Christians. Greek philosophy and religion on their long journey, led naturally toward the search for truth, wherever it was to be found. Christianity in its beginning was addressed to the Greeks, the thinkers and artists, the independent people who loved freedom. A people who, like Socrates, believed that there was in everyone a divine light which could be kindled into flame. Unfortunately, by then, the Greeks were already succumbing to the massive weight of Imperial Rome, and it was through the Romans, the strong and well-organized, the cruel and authoritative power, that Christianity developed and became a state religion. The terrors and massacres, the inquisitions, the persecutions of Christian by Christian, might never have come about if Greece and not Rome had prevailed.

In the history of the pagan world there was a long development of man's knowledge of god. The pagan gods did not come into being by the imaginative speculation about divinity by a single group of people; they arose from the coalescence of a vast number of deities, some of whom came in with different bodies of invaders during historical times, and others which had existed among the primitive inhabitants of Greece long before them. The peculiar Greek contribution to this vast array of gods was the ordering of them into a clearly defined group and the raising of their stature to the point at which they could be worshipped with dignity by an enlightened people. Every primitive local foreign god was regarded as a revelation of one or the other of the great family of gods known as the Olympian deities. The twelve Olympian gods, Hera, Zeus, Athene, Apollo, Hermes, Aphrodite, Hephaestos, Ares, Poseidon, Demeter, and Hestia, each displayed some part in the ordering of the world and in the nature of the life of man himself.

It was Homer, in about 800 B.C., the earliest storyteller and

[1] Robert Payne. *The Splendour of Greece*, 1961.

poet of all, who first displayed the gods with the clear characters they kept more or less for the next thousand years; but to him they were aristocratic rulers who managed their affairs in a way that differed very little from that of the kings who ruled on the earth in the earliest days of history. Like the mortal rulers, the gods lived a boisterous life, fighting and hunting, drinking and singing. There was an accepted standard of chivalrous conduct observed by both gods and kings, but they both had arbitrary powers over their subjects and took what they wanted whether it was cattle or women. Later philosophers were to refine and modify the idea of the gods until it was even suggested that they were all aspects of one great god.

The Greeks had no formal set of religious laws or scripture, and religion was free to live and grow; one of the more important functions of Delphi was to give guidance on religious observances and so eventually help in the development of a more exalted view of the gods. Even the most barbaric beliefs were softened and made to fit into the ordered pattern so loved by the Greeks, but, with few exceptions, they still turned to Homer for the basic concept of the great family of gods.

The greatest of the Olympian gods was Zeus. Originally a god of the sky and the weather, he eventually came to be regarded as the eternal and universal god, the creator and father. In the second century A.D. the Roman Emperor and Stoic philosopher, Marcus Aurelius, with sublime belief in the brotherhood of man, called the world 'the city of Zeus'.[1] Five hundred years earlier, men sang in hymns: 'Zeus was, Zeus is, Zeus shall be,'[2] and the poet Aratos wrote: 'From Zeus let us begin: Him do we mortals never leave un-named. Full of Zeus are all the streets and all the market places of man: full is the sea and the heavens thereof. Always we have need of Zeus: for we are his offspring.'[3]

It was Zeus the Creator, whose thoughts laid down the pattern for men's lives and whose wisdom it was best for men to follow: but the thoughts of Zeus were hidden. He was supreme, and it was impossible to approach him directly.

[1] Marcus Aurelius. *Meditations.*

[2] *Hymn of Cleanthes*, quoted by Charles Seltman in *The Twelve Olympians*, 1952.

[3] Aratos of Soloi, quoted by Charles Seltman, ibid.

Apollo was the son of Zeus and, during historical times, he became the symbol of all that was best in the outlook of the Greek spirit. He represented art and music and poetry, the love of youth and beauty and health, as well as an appreciation of the need for good government and moderation in behaviour. He was the enlightener, and among the gods he had the unique power of bringing to men foreknowledge of what was in the thoughts of Zeus; and so giving guidance about the best course for them in their affairs.

It was believed that in order to speak to men he had to find a place of communication, and so, after some dispute with the other gods jealous of his powers, he came to Delphi. A hymn that was sung in his honour says that he came down from Olympos, the mountain of the gods, and travelled south:

> And came to Krissa beneath snowy Parnassus,
> A foot-hill turned toward the west: a cliff hangs
> Over it from above, and a hollow rugged glade runs under
> There the lord Phoebus Apollo resolved to make his lovely
>   temple.[1]

It was said that at that time Delphi was occupied by a great serpent, or dragon, known as the Python, which from its dark lair guarded the powers of the oracle or prophecy possessed by Ge, the primitive goddess of the Earth. Apollo slew the dragon with his arrow and took the oracle for his own use. From then onwards, he was the Lord of Delphi and was known as the Pythian Apollo. Later he was joined by his younger brother, Dionysos, the mystic ecstatic god, a newcomer to the Olympian family, but we shall hear more of him later.

It was not by chance that Apollo chose Delphi, there were many reasons why it was the right home for the god. It is one of the most beautiful places in Greece and has a majesty which makes it a fit setting for a temple. The Greeks appreciated beauty in nature as well as in art and their appreciation had a religious impact. They agreed that, if a thing was holy and good, it should be as beautiful as possible; every temple they built owed much of its architectural beauty to its relationship with its surroundings. Apollo also chose Delphi because it

[1] *Homeric Hymn*, quoted by Charles Seltman, ibid.

was thought to be the true centre of the world, and so placed that it was the focus of all the world's activities; but most important of all was the fact that it already contained those strange influences and magic forces which brought prophetic powers to whoever passed by. Stone-Age man, before he knew anything of the Olympian gods, felt the mysterious power of the earth itself acting there and, even after Apollo had come, the men who slept in Delphi were for a long time disturbed by strange dreams. Euripides in 414 B.C. described how the dreams . . .

> . . . from deep confused underworlds of sleep
> They showed blind things that erst had been and are,
> and yet shall follow.[1]

The god Apollo, using the powers that already existed in Delphi, spoke through his own priestess and gave those oracles, or messages of guidance to men, which were to enlighten them through so many years of Greek, and later, Roman history.

As the fame of the oracle spread, Delphi in its isolated mountainous setting became an important place, and for many years it not only answered the queries of humble seekers for help, but decided the political life of whole nations.

Around the lovely temple of Apollo grew a city which was never large but of very great renown. For more than a thousand years the inquirers came here to consult the oracle, and to worship the god who filled the whole precinct with the power and terror of his presence. In his honour they brought gifts and the dedication of their most precious possessions, and the small city of Delphi became the richest and most famous religious centre of the Greek world.

[1] Euripides. *Iphigenia in Tauris*. Translated by Gilbert Murray, 1910.

THE Greeks have never been a single people with a simple common racial origin, and there has always been a great diversity of race and custom among them. The mainland of Greece is divided by the mountains and an irregular coastline, and farther away still lie the islands, each with its own character and local traditions. With poor communications across the natural barriers, it is understandable how there developed a form of government in which there were many individual city-states, or 'poleis'. Each polis included the land around a city, with the farms and villages, and it was independent and self-sufficient. From time to time there were coalitions and loose forms of agreement between these states, but often there were bitter feuds and wars. It was only in times of great national emergency that they united in any great number to fight a common enemy. As a state prospered and was unable to expand within its own territory, it sent colonists to found a new city in the barbarian lands on distant shores of the Mediterranean. A colony in its turn, in spite of traditional links with its mother city, nearly always became independent and took its part in the feuds and rivalries between groups of states.

In spite of the differences in outlook, and political systems which ranged from despotic rule by kings and dictators to the most extreme forms of democracy, there was a consciousness that something united them and made them Greeks, and so, different from barbarians. This was partly because, in spite of local dialects, they shared a common language. It is comparatively recently that Greece was confined within clear national boundaries, and wherever Greek is spoken, is in one sense, a part of Greece. Perhaps more important than language, was the unity in a shared religion, and an attitude to life which that religion produced. In the stories of Homer, the gods took sides with various warring factions, and often provoked disputes to satisfy their own quarrels and jealousies, but as ideas changed, the gods became a source of unity. This was felt most intensely in Delphi, which played its finest role as a place in which Greeks found this knowledge of a common tradition.

Besides being a place of oracle and the home of Apollo, Delphi was also an art gallery and a shrine where every important event in the history of the Greeks was commemorated by paintings and sculptures.

Each of the states sent its greatest artists to Delphi to display works which were representative of their own particular culture and every period in history. They sent the most beautiful of their products and their most precious gifts and offerings. At Delphi the bitter rivalries on the battlefields, became a rivalry to proclaim the greatest achievements of each people in order to impress friends and allies, as well as enemies.

There was no generally accepted formula or special style to which the artists had to conform, and each strove to produce the finest work he could, as an expression of the culture of his native city. Where possible he brought from his homeland the stone and metal on which to work. The many styles of the Greek world were maintained in a pure form at Delphi making the sanctuary unique. Only here, was there a complete display of the range of Greek artistic genius. Messelière, the French archaeologist, said: 'Delphi is the microcosm of a total Greece. One might prefer the "force" of the Dorians, the Ionian "grace" or the Attic "measure", but any one is not more Hellenic than another; none of them alone represents the best of Hellenism; none of them was without fault, without the others they were not in equilibrium. Without its whole support the Tripod is not balanced and it falls.'[1]

After working at Delphi, the artists returned home, newly inspired by the sight of the work of others. New ideas were developed to improve the standards of their own people and so, like a leaven, the spirit of Delphi spread, to create a brilliance in art which was truly pan-Hellenic.

Poets and musicians as well as painters and sculptors competed at Delphi, and it was said that the muses, the nine spirits which inspired the creative arts of men, who had formerly lived farther away on Mount Helikon, came to live on Parnassos, sure of a welcome from Apollo.

The sacred enclosure at Delphi was more than just an art

[1] P. de la Cost-Messelière. *Delphes*, 1943.

gallery, however; it was here at the religious and political focus of the pan-Hellenic world that all the triumphs in war and peace of the individual states were recorded, in monuments and trophies, that often revealed the intense rivalry that divided them, when away from the sanctuary. At Delphi they felt a profound joy in sharing what seemed to be a manifestation of a superior civilization; the symbol of what it meant to be Greek. It was the centre of a common heritage of a people so diverse in some ways, and yet united in the confidence that by the sacred fire burning on the high altar, they were brothers.

Apollo was the god of harmony and ordered government, who spoke wisely to the worshippers who gathered at his temple, but he was continually misinterpreted or ignored. There was too often a savage betrayal of the noble principles Apollo represented in the hierarchy of the gods, and this eventually led to the heroic yet tragic end of the power of the Greeks, after the unsurpassed glory of their past. Looking back on Greek history in the year A.D. 80, Plutarch wrote sadly, about the monuments at Delphi: 'She erected nearly all her trophies to her own shame and misery and was brought to ruin and desolation almost wholly by the guilt and ambition of her great men.'[1]

Parnassos has not changed. It is still as wild and as lovely as ever; the air is still as keen as when Plutarch described it, and to those who are sufficiently dedicated, there is still inspiration to be found at Delphi. Little, however, remains of its greatest glories. Part of the site is known as the Marmaria, 'the marble quarry', which significantly points to man's destructive power. The remainder of the city and the sacred enclosure was taken back by the earth as the winter storms brought mud and stones from the mountainside and covered it completely. Excavations are now revealing more and more of Delphi's splendours, but to know how it looked before it was lost, we must turn to the traveller Pausanias.

We are very fortunate that almost the whole of the famous *Description of Greece* by Pausanias has survived. He wrote and travelled between A.D. 145 and 180 when the greatest glory of Greece had long departed, but at a time when there was a last revival of her fortunes under the influence of Roman emperors like Hadrian and Marcus Aurelius, who admired Greece as the

[1] Plutarch. *Moralia.*

home of culture and religion. There were many earlier historians and writers who spoke at length of Delphi. Pausanias' journey through Greece, however, was not as a historian, but as a tourist, who observed with interest and curiosity all that he heard and saw on his travels, and wrote his impressions as a guide for other travellers. So accurate and careful are these descriptions, that his books held their place as the standard guide to Greece both for the classical scholar and the archaeologist for more than 1,700 years.

When Pausanias came to Delphi it was still a city to be wondered at. Under the hot sun, reflected from the glowing mountain walls, the buildings shone with white marble. The inner walls of the temples and arcades were painted in pastel colours, pink, blue and green—the colours which were used so effectively by the ancient Greeks to show off the perfect contours of pillars and carved stone. The bronze statues and monuments, and even some of the ancient stonework, already had the patina of delicate blue and green for which Delphi was famous, as Plutarch once remarked when discussing with his friends the effects of the air on the metal and stonework. Although the gold is missing which adorned the statue of the charioteer, in the museum at Delphi, it once shone against the green metal, in the open sunlight, and the artists and craftsmen of those days were well aware that nature could add even more beauty to their workmanship. The graceful buildings of the treasuries and art galleries, gymnasiums and temples, the fountains and porticoes, as well as more modest houses and hotels, were all built with an elegance suitable for the adornment of the holy city.

On the crest of the slope above the city, within the area of the sanctuary, were the greatest works of art to be found anywhere in the world at that time, but dominating everything, above the city and sanctuary, was the mighty temple of Apollo. Although some of the greatest treasures had already been plundered, and the treasuries for storing the most valuable gifts stood empty when Pausanias went to Delphi, the great temple itself had been recently restored and life in the city was as busy as it ever had been. The Greeks were interested in the careful preservation of ancient remains and objects of historical significance, in a way that has only been paralleled in our own time, and everywhere he went Pausanias was shown venerated relics of more ancient days, and heard the stories and legends about them told by guides and curators. Like many Greek writers he was shrewdly sceptical about the more improbable stories, but this was tempered by respect for the wisdom that he felt lay hidden beneath them.

From his vivid descriptions we can now identify the remains of buildings; we can trace the sacred path winding its way up to the temple, and visualize the time when there were so many monuments and statues that Delphi was called the 'forest of marble'.

The greatest art treasures originally displayed at Delphi have nearly all gone. A few survived, and are in the Delphi Museum, but these are among the least celebrated of the masterpieces presented to the sanctuary by different Greek states. Once the sanctuary held the finest works of all the most famous artists of the ancient world, but now almost nothing is left; except for those few things preserved by the accidents of time and weather.

Although what we can see now was only mentioned in passing, if at all, by ancient visitors to Delphi, who were so enthusiastic about the other rare and beautiful works, we are grateful that enough remains to recapture for us something of the skill and vision of their creators. The best known of the statues in the museum at Delphi is the Charioteer, which was not even mentioned by Pausanias, and now occupies a place of honour.

Today, Delphi is more famous for its Charioteer, which we can examine so closely and with so much wonder, than for the oracle that was once supreme. He stands alone now, as he never stood when he was first placed among the other monuments that surrounded the temple. The grave figure in the long rippling robe, with its pale green patina seldom fails to excite and delight visitors. He is very young, with an expression on his face that is aristocratic and stern, and yet with the feeling that it will break into a smile at any moment, to reveal all the humanity and vigorous life of the youth.

To us the most precious feature of this bronze statue is that, in its perfect preservation, it is really the best example we have of the fully modelled workmanship of a sculptor as it left his studio. The weather-worn Greek statues, with blank eyes, that are found in museums throughout the world, have so impressed us with their beauty that there has arisen a fear that in their original form, with added colour and carefully modelled eyes, the beauty of the sculpture might have become banal and garish and our respect for Greek artistic taste lessened in some way. The face of the Charioteer has reassured us that, even in the careful details of life added by the sculptor, there was no descent to the level of the wax model, and the sure sense of incomparable artistic beauty was never lost.

The features are finely modelled and the hair, which is engraved, lies in formal curls close to the head, held in place by a band, once encrusted with gold. The lips were once inlaid with red copper, and the teeth, just visible, were represented by a strip of silver, but it is the eyes that give such an illusion of life. The whites are of enamel paste, set with black pupils in brown onyx, and each eyelash, above and below the eye, is carefully chiselled from thin bronze.

The technical workmanship is astonishing, and is in what is known as the lost wax process. Although the style is archaic in some respects, there is a use and control of archaic elements which show a superb mastery of every complexity of design. The torso is not highly modelled and the long tunic, with its twenty-one deep folds, every one different, is stiff and yet full of hidden movement. The unseen threads which gather it can be sensed under the material, as it flows across the arms and shoulders.

It is the feet which are so often recommended to us, as every muscle and its tension is flawlessly represented, and we are told that high on a pedestal and enclosed in a chariot they would never have been seen by human eyes. They are a supreme gesture of the integrity of the sculptor. Archaeologists believe that the Charioteer, represented in bronze, was part of a large group of statues. Fragments of horses' legs and hooves and bronze reins were found near it, together with the arm of a child that may have stood at the side of the Charioteer. Part of the stone base bears the name *Polyzalos*, assumed to be the younger brother of Gelon, Tyrant of Syracuse, who was victorious in a chariot race in 486 B.C. The young Charioteer may have been depicted driving in the ceremonial procession, that followed his victory, but this has been disputed. The pieces of chariot may have no connection with our Charioteer. It is certain that he is a noble youth, and he has all the bearing of a Sicilian prince, but he may also have represented another of the familiar images of Apollo, and have stood alone where he could have been seen at eye-level, in all his beauty.

We can only imagine the still more beautiful works that once adorned the sanctuary. Pausanias wrote: 'I will enumerate all the votive offerings that are best worthy of mention. The athletes, however, and musical competitors of no great merit, I do not think worthy of attention.'[1]

He passed the treasuries of the Syphnians and Athenians, as if they were quite bare of sculptural adornment, only mentioning in each case by whom they were dedicated. There is no comment on the Sphinx of the Naxians, or the group of the statues on the monument of Daochus, the remains of which are preserved in the museum today, and it is obvious that what is left for us to wonder at is only a reflection of the light that shone from Delphi when it was the most radiant place in the world.

The Sphinx of the Naxians crouches on the remains of the capital of a pillar. Its damaged stone reveals little of how it must have looked when it was first erected high in the air, as an offering in 570 B.C., but Plutarch said: 'When the sphinx was seen against the sun's rays the animal's back was of golden hue; but, when standing against the clouds, it threw back a dark blue reflection just like a rainbow.'[2]

The friezes and decorations of the treasuries, which Pausanias did not mention, now make up the greater part of the sculptures of the museum, and though they may have been of small importance we are grateful that we can admire them now. Some of the broken pieces are still being patiently put together in the workshops of the French archaeologists, and some are almost complete or reconstructed in plaster. Unlike many of the monuments glorifying the deeds of historical times, the decoration of the treasuries all show legendary heroes and gods. The treasury of Sikyon, sculptured in the sixth century B.C., tells stories familiar to every Greek child. There is the rape of Europa by the divine bull. Zeus saw Europa, the daughter of a Phoenician king, plucking flowers in a meadow and fell in love with her. 'He descended, changed himself into a bull, and

1 Pausanias. *Description of Greece*, Phokis. Translated by A. R. Shilleto, 1886.
2 Plutarch. *Moralia*.

breathed perfume from his mouth. . . .' Another part of the frieze tells the story of the hunt of the Kalydonian Boar, which destroyed vineyards, killing cattle and men. A third section shows the ship of the Argonauts with its equipment.

The Siphnian treasury was probably the oldest marble building on the Greek mainland, and had caryatids supporting its portico. Most of the frieze is still preserved and once again shows a whole gallery of famous stories—the judgement of Paris, the Trojan Wars, the conflict of the gods and giants—among others. Two different sculptors worked on this frieze, and the difference in style can still be seen. One is described as lyrical, the other as epic.

The Athenian treasury was no different. Here can be seen Herakles at his labours, Theseus fighting the Minotaur and a whole company of Amazons on galloping horses, but perhaps of greatest interest to us now is the only surviving example of a hymn, accompanied by ancient musical notation. This is inscribed on a wall of the treasury where it can still be clearly seen, but its interpretation has puzzled generations of musicians anxious to know more about the music of ancient Greece.

Among the statues that were dedicated in the sanctuary it is only natural that a large number were of Apollo, and these statues represented every artistic period from the remote archaic to the classical times. Out of twenty groups of statues referred to by Pausanias in one part of the sanctuary, eleven were of Apollo, seven alone and four together in a group, and one of them was over sixty feet high. A little farther along he saw a row of twenty Apollos, lined up on each side of the path. This was a single offering by the Liparians. The oracle had advised them how to attack a number of Tyrrhenian pirates, and with only five ships they captured twenty of those of the enemy. For every captured ship they erected an Apollo.

Apart from the statues of Apollo, countless other figures were portrayed, isolated or in groups. Statues of Olympic gods, local kings and heroes were displayed, among them the founders and ancestors of different Greek peoples; Andreus, in a 'coat of mail with a cloak over it', the founder of the island of Andros; Aetolia 'an armed woman' from the Aetolians, and many others. The barbarians who came to Delphi imitated this custom: 'Of the western barbarians the Sardinians offered a brazen statue of Sardus from whom their Island took its name,' and Pausanias mentions in passing that on Sardinia was a deadly grass like parsley, that made men die of laughter if they ate it, and was the origin of the expression 'sardonic laughter'.

Later in the history of Delphi there came portrait statues of kings and powerful men that the cities hastened to honour, in particular the Roman Emperors.

Some of the monuments were more elaborate and original than others. There was the portico holding the figureheads and bronze shields captured by the Athenians, and another Athenian memorial in the form of a bronze palm tree with representations of fruit and owls, which had a gilded statue of Athene standing on it. In the sixth century B.C., the Orneans of Argolis vowed that they would arrange to have a sacrificial procession at Delphi every day if they were delivered from the enemies who were invading the country. 'They obtained the wished-for victory but as to discharge their vow daily was a great expense, they hit upon the expedient of offering to the god representations in brass of the procession and sacrifice.'[1]

In the following century the Argives displayed bronze figures of captured horses and barbarian women all fettered with chains.

It was the ironwork that Pausanias particularly admired, not because of its beauty but because 'making statues in iron is most difficult and laborious'. There was a representation in iron of one of the labours of Herakles by a designer called Tisagoras, and also the iron base of the bowl presented by Alyattes, the father of Croesus the Lydian king, which was the first known example of welding. This was made by a Greek named Glaucus from the island of Chios. Pausanias says: 'The places where the base is joined are not rivetted together by bolts or nails, but simply by welding. This base, from a broad bottom rises turret-like to a point. The sides are not entirely covered, but have girders of iron like the steps of a ladder. Straight bars of iron bend outwards at the extremities and this is the seat for the bowl.'[2] The silver bowl itself had been stolen long before, but the guardians of Delphi had preserved the perishable iron base for nearly 700 years when Pausanias marvelled at it.

[1] Pausanias. *Description of Greece.*
[2] Ibid.

One of the most beautiful of all the statues admired by Pausanias shone rather scandalously among the solemn kings and heroes. This was of the courtesan, Phryne. According to Pausanias: 'The gilt statue of Phryne here was made by Praxiteles, one of her lovers, and was an offering of Phryne herself.'[1]

The famous Hermes of Praxiteles survives today in the museum of Olympia, and from it we can judge how beautiful the statue of Phryne would have appeared, made as it was by someone about whom a Greek chronicler wrote: 'Who gave a soul to marble? Who put into stone the ardent desire for pleasure? It was done by Praxiteles.'

Alongside the gods and heroes were many statues of animals, particularly horses. Owners of horses, winning races at the games, would commission a famous bronzesmith to make a 'quadriga' or four-horse team. The Charioteer is believed to have been a part of one of these groups. The Argives sent a bronze horse in imitation of the horse of Troy after a battle with the Lacedaemonians. It was considered a drawn battle, but the Argives wanted it recorded that they thought 'they had got the best of it'. The Athenian, Kallias, gained so much personal loot from the war with the Persians, that he made a private offering of a horse. Apart from the many horses, there were other animals, a bronze bull offered by the people of Korkyra in return for a miraculous haul of tunny fish; several goats, one of them from the people of Kleonae in thankfulness for their delivery from plague, and 'the brazen head of the Paeonian bison' from the Paeonians who tamed wild bison for their own use. Near the great altar outside the temple was the wolf, offered by the Delphians themselves.

Tradition said that a thief stole some of the gold of the sanctuary: '. . . and hid himself in that part of Parnassus where the forest trees were most thick, and that a wolf attacked him and killed him, and that this wolf used to run into the town daily and howl, and the Delphians thought this could not be but divine direction, so they followed the wolf and discovered the sacred gold, and offered to the god a bronze wolf'.[2] There was even a statue of a donkey that had pursued a she-ass, with loud

[1] Pausanias. *Description of Greece.*
[2] Ibid.

braying, and so saved the Ambraciotes from an ambush prepared for them.

When Pausanias went to Delphi, many of the offerings were missing through the plunder of armies and robbers. '. . . And last of all, it was fated to experience Nero's contempt of everything, for he carried off from Apollo 500 brazen statues, some of gods, some of men.' The new statues of Roman emperors, were little recompense for the things which were lost.

Pausanias entered Delphi by what was once the gate of the city, near the temple of Athene Pronaia, by what is now known as the Marmaria. He said: 'As you enter Delphi there are four temples in a row, the first in ruins, the next without statues or effigies, the third had a few of the Roman emperors, the fourth called the temple of Athene Pronaia.' He had little to say about this area, but the round Tholos, built by the architect Theodorus, and now partly reconstructed, is one of the loveliest parts of the sanctuary, and we now know that the temple of Athene Pronaia is the site of the most ancient cult of Delphi, for Athene succeeded the original Mycenaean goddess, who once reigned at Delphi.

One small statue that Pausanias regretted had been stolen by Nero was of Hydna. After the Persian wars, the Amphictionic Council erected a special statue to 'Scyllis, who had wonderful fame as a diver, and taught his daughter, Hydna, diving. When a violent storm came on Xerxes' fleet off Mount Pelion they greatly added to the wrecks by diving down and cutting the cables that kept the ships at anchor. It was for this good service that the Amphictions made the statues of Scyllis and his daughter.'

In describing this early frogman's feat, Pausanias added the remarkable statement that: 'Virgins that are virgins indeed still dive in the sea with impunity.'

Pausanias walked along the road past the gymnasium and the swimming baths, that today form a shady grove of olive trees, past the spring of Kastalia in its deep gorge to the entrance to the sanctuary.

The Sacred Way, which wound up to the temple is still there, but only broken stones of pediments line the paved pathway. Here, near the entrance, the Athenian statues made by Phidias, the sculptor of the Parthenon, looked across at their enemies,

c

the Lacedaemonian sailors, who glared back at them. In the time of Plutarch these old bronze statues were covered with a beautiful blue patina, so that people spoke of them as true blue sailors. Once they were decorated with gold stars but, as they in their turn were defeated, the gold stars disappeared and were never seen again. Now the rivalry between the Athenians and the Lacedaemonians, so publicly proclaimed, is ended by the hand of time, which, showing no preference, has obliterated both groups of statues.

The sacred path led up past the treasuries, the statues and monuments to the front of the temple, where in a great paved area the tremendous altar of Apollo stood, which is now partly reconstructed.

Pausanias did not enter the temple, where the golden statue of Apollo and the holiest objects of the sanctuary, the *omphalos* and tripod, were kept, but turned to the building on the hillside, at the side of the theatre, which was of particular interest to him. This was the Lesche, or the clubhouse, where the people of Delphi used to gather to meet their friends and to talk. This building was one of the glories of Delphi, as here were the paintings of the artist Polygnotus.

The colours of the great paintings of the Greek world have long been lost, and we can only speculate, from the designs on pottery how they may have appeared. The fame of the great mural painters like Polygnotus in the fifth century B.C. was very great, and if the quality of the sculptured works which have survived is any criterion, the paintings would have been yet another example of the Greek artistic genius.

The mural painting in the Lesche was a splendid display of the story of the Trojan War, and the descent into Hades by Odysseus. More than 150 characters appeared, including all the famous names in legend and history of those days. From Pausanias' description, the scene was portrayed in vivid detail. On one wall were the ships and soldiers; Trojan women 'in sad dejection as if they were captives already'; the terrified children clinging to the altars, as the soldiers fought and died at the walls of Troy; and all the rest of the drama of Homer's *Iliad*. On the opposite wall, Charon ferried Odysseus across the river where the 'fishes are so indistinct that they look like ghosts of fishes', into the land of Hades. Here he met all the legendary figures of the past who lived as unhappy shades in the under-world. Here too there were demons like Eurynomus, who ate the flesh of the dead. He was 'blue-ish black, like the flies that infest meat, and he shows his fangs, and sits on a vulture's skin'. Pausanias examined the pictures with great interest, and not uncritically. He remarked that there was a horse rolling in the dust on the sea-shore . . . 'You can see the pebbles, but the rest of the scene doesn't look much like a sea-view.'

In spite of all the drama and solemnity of the historical pageant, Polygnotus still managed to add a little humour. Oknus, a friend of Odysseus, 'is represented rope-making, and a she-ass near him eats the rope as fast as he makes it. This Oknus, they say, was an industrious man, who had an extrava-gant wife; and whatever he got together by industry was very soon spent by her.'

Now, only a few stones of the Lesche remain to remind us of the time when, after watching a play performed by some group of travelling actors, the audience would stroll along to the club-house, so conveniently placed near the back of the theatre, to talk and laugh about the latest comedy or farce. They were not just a provincial audience in a small city far away from the active world outside. Sometimes, when the oracle was not functioning and no festivals were taking place, Delphi was quiet enough, but always there was the knowledge that it was the centre of the world. When the crowds gathered, they came to the venerable place which was the very heart of the nation's culture.

Pericles was speaking of Athens in 430 B.C., when he said: 'Mighty indeed are the marks and monuments of our empire which we have left. Future ages will wonder at us, as the present age wonders at us now.'[1] Even more might this be said of Delphi. Athens had her own monuments, and happily so many of them have survived, but Delphi displayed in one place the works of the whole, scattered Greek world.

[1] Thucydides. *Peloponnesian War*, Pericles' funeral speech. Translated by Rex Warner, 1954.

3 · *Pythia*

AMONG the sanctuaries of the pagan gods, Delphi was unique because of the oracle. In most of the great sanctuaries and temples there were departments of divination; the priests found it added to the wealth and popularity of a shrine if it gave help and guidance to followers who sought to know what the gods had in store for them. In Delphi the oracle was there from the beginning and it was deliberately chosen by the god as a place of revelation. Everything in Delphi is prepared for the gods to communicate with mortals. Suspended between air and earth, in a curve of the shining walls of the mountain, the most distant whisper of life is magnified and concentrated on the sacred focus of the world. It is said that in the beginning Zeus the creator sent two eagles, each from the uttermost ends of the earth, and it was here that they met, at the earth's veritable centre. The air here is full of omens; and the storms and thunderbolts of winter and the eagles of Zeus still glide and soar round the sanctuary.

Diodorus, who lived in the first century B.C. tells a legendary story that in the remote past there was a chasm in the rocks at the spot where later the temple was built. Goatherds tended their flocks on the mountainside then, just as they do today, and it happened that one of them called Koretas discovered the great fissure. To his amazement the goats began to tremble violently and to jump about. They began to bleat in a very odd way. Koretas naturally peered over the edge of the chasm to see what had disturbed them, and then he also began to talk in a strange manner, and to prophesy. The other goatherds, who were following behind him, decided that there was some miraculous power here, and that the inspiration came from Mother Earth herself. Diodorus goes on to say:

For some time those who wished to consult the prophetic power of the oracle, prophesied for each other. Eventually, as many of them had fallen into the chasm under the influence of the emanation and had

24

without exception disappeared, it seemed proper to the inhabitants of the region in order to protect themselves from the dangers, to elect a woman as unique prophetess for all of them. They built a platform on which she climbed, and from which in complete security she could receive the inspiration. The platform had three supports and was therefore given the name of Tripod.[1]

As with so many of the legends collected by Roman writers, this one was a popular fallacy and we must look to other accounts to discover what the consultation was really like, and these can tell us a great deal.

Towards the end of its long history, there lived a man with a personal interest in the temple of Apollo, whose name will always be linked with Delphi; this was Plutarch.

Plutarch was born in Chaeronea, a small town in central Greece, in the year A.D. 45. He was a historian and philosopher, gentle and learned, and most of his readers have loved and respected his character as it is revealed in his writing. Nine hundred years after his death, when William the Conqueror was invading England, a bishop of the Byzantine Church prayed: 'If, Lord, Thou art willing in Thy grace to save any Pagans from the wrath of God, I pray Thee humbly to save Plato and Plutarch.'[2]

As one of the most respected men of his day, he was appointed high priest of Apollo at Delphi, and he wrote lovingly about the solemn affairs of the temple. During his lifetime the material power of the Greeks was completely finished, and an age of superstition and corruption existed throughout the Roman Empire to which Greece then belonged. To Plutarch, and a few enlightened men, it was a time when the expression of pagan beliefs in god was at its finest, and yet the oracle of Apollo was failing and a new religious age was on the horizon. Plutarch saw in the failing powers of the oracle, a sign of the lack of faith of men. The working of the oracle, the inspired speech and the writing of sacred books, were all done through men who were instruments that could fail, but the power of God remained. 'God is not a ventriloquist,' Plutarch firmly declared.

[1] Diodorus Siculus. *World History*: XVI. 26. Translated by Charles L. Sherman, 1952.
[2] Quoted by Edith Hamilton in *The Echo of Greece*.

From his writings, so many of which have been preserved, we know a great deal about the ceremonial that had to be observed by those who came to consult the oracle, and the mystery which surrounded the power of the Pythia, the priestess through whom the oracles were delivered. He also wrote about the organization of the sanctuary and its traditions.

The oracle was not available at every time that anyone wanted to consult it. Although answers were given at more frequent intervals in later days, there was always a strict control over their times. At first, after it had become the home of Apollo, the oracle only responded once a year. This was at the end of February on the seventh day of Bysios, the anniversary of Apollo's birthday. Later as the sanctuary grew in importance it was usual to hold a session once a month during nine months of the year. Plutarch says that it was only possible 'to enclose the god in a mortal body once a month'. During very busy times, consultations might have been made more than once a month for important visitors, but they were always strictly forbidden on certain days.[1] In particular these were during the three winter months when Apollo was away from the shrine and no oracles were possible.

The sanctuary was a particularly busy place during the festivals, held every four years in August, and visitors came from all over the Hellenic world. Sometimes in a single day, as many as fifty thousand people passed through Kirra, the port which once existed near Itea. It was not necessary, of course, to go to the oracle personally to make a consultation, and many cities and rulers had their own special arrangements at Delphi. Often a request for some special service was sent by courier in written form. Aesop, when he went to Delphi, was said to be the courier of Croesus, King of Lydia.

In Athens there lived representatives of the Delphic Apollo who advised on matters concerning the oracle. According to an inscription found in Athens, on at least one occasion they recommended that the Athenian Assembly should send a written request for guidance to Delphi. The query concerned the arrangements for the cultivation of the sacred plain of Eleusis, a matter of some concern to the landowners involved.

[1] *Nefaste*, the Latin word commonly used, is not strictly correct, referring as it does to sacred days on which legal business could not take place.

The Assembly agreed that on a religious matter of this kind the decision should be made by Apollo at Delphi. Two statements were prepared, one negative and the other affirmative, and these were engraved on two similar sheets of tin. The sheets were rolled up, wrapped in woollen cloth and placed in a bronze jar. The jar was shaken and then the packages were drawn out one at a time. The first was put into a gold vessel and the second into one of silver, and three couriers carried them to Delphi. The oracle was asked to indicate which of the two vessels contained the correct answer to the Athenian problem.

When it was essential that no hint of interference by the interested parties to a dispute must exist, the greatest secrecy was necessary.[1] Usually there was no secrecy about the nature of a question and the Spartans, especially, appeared to be particularly naïve about publicizing their plans when they intended to invade a neighbouring territory.

Many inquirers consulted the oracle personally, and of course there were many others who went to Delphi simply as pilgrims visiting the sanctuary. Sometimes they came across the pass from central Greece, following the route taken by the modern road, through Arachova. Ordinary people made the long journey on foot, but the older and richer clients came in chariots with slaves and attendants. Oedipus describes how he met and killed his father, Laius, who was returning from Delphi: 'When I came to the place where three roads join, I met a herald followed by a horse-drawn carriage, and a man seated therein, just as you have described.'[2] The place where the three roads join, on the road to Delphi, is still pointed out to visitors, although now the motor road bypasses the fatal cross-roads. An important man like King Laius not only had four attendants, but a herald to assist in his journey to a sacred place like Delphi, and even in war-torn Greece the herald was usually respected. In the fight which started when the attendants thrust Oedipus aside, the king and three others were killed. Oedipus was not aware that the man he had killed was his father and he went on to fulfil the terrible prophecy given by the Delphic Oracle, that he would kill his own father and marry his own mother.

[1] Shakespeare was aware of this method of consulting the oracle, probably from Plutarch. Cf. *The Winter's Tale*: Act III, scene II.
[2] Sophocles. *King Oedipus*. Translated by E. F. Watling, 1947.

Many of the visitors came by sea through the Gulf of Corinth and would walk up the steep path to Delphi from the port of Kirra near the modern Itea. It was a pleasant walk in summer, but in early spring and autumn the pilgrims would be glad to wrap their woollen cloaks around them as the bitter winds blew down the mountainsides. Many of them would be barefoot, although boots and sandals were worn. Socrates boasted that he had remained barefoot when he served in the citizen army on the mountain campaigns. Even today it is wild country round Parnassos, and in those days when there were strict laws against cultivation in the valley, which is now a sea of olive trees, it must have been even more barren. It would have been a dramatic moment to reach the top of the path and to come suddenly on the city of Delphi, shining with white marble and limestone, on its mountain ledge. I have no doubt that pilgrims would sing a Paean to honour the sacred city as they first saw it. Paeans were the hymns that were especially dedicated to Apollo and the sound of the word *paean* was said to imitate the song of the god's arrows as they flew through the air from his golden bow.

On arriving at Delphi, the visitor would probably seek out the representative of his city, for most city-states kept a permanent ambassador at Delphi who acted as a sponsor for his own countrymen. Strangers were never permitted to consult the oracle unless special arrangements were made for them to be sponsored. Some people had the advantage of being given the freedom of Delphi, because of their special relationship with Apollo; in particular there were the followers of Asklepios from Kos. Sometimes this privilege was granted, as it was to Croesus, in return for some particular generosity.

Even when they had not come to consult the oracle itself, Delphi was a fascinating place for visitors. In the darkness of the warm summer evenings there would be much discussion in the squares and porticoes and, as happened at all great sanctuaries, there would be guides and soothsayers and sellers of religious objects clamouring for custom. For the energetic there were the gymnasiums and swimming baths, and for others, schools of rhetoric and organized lectures.

Although the oracle was, of course, the most important function of Delphi, other means of divination were not neglected,

The Delphic Sibyl. Fresco by Michelangelo in the Sistine Chapel.
Among the prophets believed to have foretold the coming of Christ was
the Pythia, here shown as a young girl. Chosen from one of the most
honest and respectable families, she always lived an irreproachable life.
Foto Anderson

Here lies Delphi, suspended in space over the valley of the Pleistos, exposed to wind and light, one of the most venerated places in the world.

From the foot of the
Phaedriades the ground falls
away steeply down to the bed
of the Pleistos, and on this
difficult slope a city was once
built.

The temple of Apollo. Some pillars were re-erected in 1941 to make it possible to envisage the general scale of the sanctuary.

The well-preserved stairway
to the theatre.

The west end of the temple.
The vast area of fallen walls
and piled masonry surrounds
the temple on every side.

The Sacred Way. Here, near the entrance, the Athenian statues glared across at their enemies, the Lacedaemonians, but now only the pediments remain. The steps were added in Roman times to prevent the sacrilegious entry of chariots.

The theatre, in its magnificent setting, was built during the fourth century B.C. It was restored in Roman times and is still very well preserved. Greek Tragedy was revived here by Sikelianos in 1927.

and private inquirers would often use the services of minor priests, who would interpret omens for them by the more usual means common in those days. Many small arguments were settled in Delphi, it is believed, without consulting the oracle at all, as the very situation so near the home of Apollo helped to produce wise decisions.

The inquirer who seriously intended to make a consultation had to observe the regulations. The two essential conditions were the offering of a victim and the consecration of a pelanos.

Originally the pelanos was a soft cake made with white flour and honey mixed with oil and water (perhaps not unlike the halva of today) which was burnt on the high altar, or presented to the priests who burnt a part of it. In later times the inquirer paid a fee, which varied according to his status, in place of the pelanos, which was then provided by the officiating priests.

The offering of a victim was a more serious matter. Usually it was a female goat and on the success of the sacrifice of the goat depended the whole working of the oracle. If the sacrifice was unsuccessful, the oracular procedure had to be cancelled. In all parts of Greece it was usual in the case of the animal sacrifices to insist that the victim should nod its head as a sign that it agreed to accept its role, but, in Delphi, Plutarch says:

No oracle is given if the victim does not tremble and shake throughout its whole body, right to the extremity of its hooves, while it is dedicated. It does not suffice if it shakes its head as with other sacrifices, it is necessary that all its members shiver and shake together with a rattling noise. In default of these signs it is declared that the Oracle does not function, and the Pythia is not introduced to it.[1]

It was not only essential to make certain that the god consented to give audience, but to approach him with humility. The god's word could not be coerced from him, and it had to be accepted in the manner he chose to give it. As it says in the *Hymn to Hermes*: 'Anyone who comes, under fallacious signs, in order to consult my oracle unreasonably and knowing that the gods are always aware of their purpose, to them I say, you take a vain journey.'[2]

[1] Plutarch. *Moralia*. On the Pythian Responses.
[2] *Homeric Hymn*. Quoted by Messelière in *Delphes*.

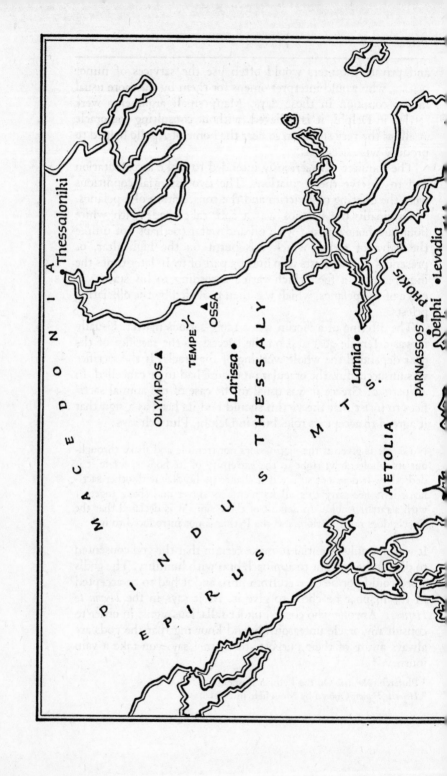

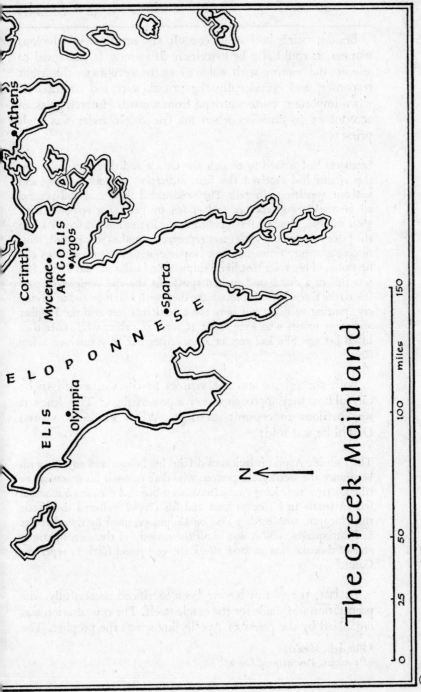

The Greek Mainland

© CASSELL & CO. LTD. 1967

0   25   50   100   150
        miles

N

Besides being useless to consult the oracle in a frivolous manner, it could also be extremely dangerous. It was usual to anoint the victim with cold water to encourage the right responses, and occasionally the priests were too enthusiastic when important visitors arrived from abroad. Plutarch gives an account of an occasion when his friend Nikander was high priest:

Strangers had arrived to consult the Oracle and they were told that the victim had received the first dedication without moving and without appearing affected. They redoubled their zeal and pressed on emulating one another and ended by getting a response with great trouble. Now what happened to the Pythia? She descended into the place of prophecy with great repugnance, and as we are told, with discouragement. From her first response it was manifest from the harshness of her voice that like a shipwrecked sailor she was adrift. She was full of a dumb and malign spirit. At the end completely confused, she threw herself through the door with a strange and terrifying cry, putting to flight not only the consultants but also the Prophet and those priests who were there. Returning a short while later they lifted her up. She had regained her senses but only survived a few days.[1]

Both the priests and the visitors to the shrine had to be careful how they approached such a powerful god. They knew it was perilous to commit sacrilege. When Pausanias visited Delphi he was told:

The Delphic Apollo is quick to defend his honour and to visit with vengeance the sacrilegious persons who dare to assail his sanctuary or rifle his treasures. King Archidamus who fingered the sacred moneys, fell in battle in a foreign land and his corpse weltered unburied; the Phlegyan, who made a raid on Delphi perished by thunderbolts and earthquakes; and it was in all the majesty of thunder, lightning and earthquake that at later times the god stood forth to repel the Gauls.[2]

At last, the victim having been sacrificed successfully, the preparation was made for the oracle itself. The consultation was organized by the priest of Apollo, known as the prophet. The

[1] Plutarch. *Moralia.*
[2] Pausanias. *Description of Greece.*

prophet was sometimes a great noble of Delphi and at other times a famous and learned man chosen for the post. He was assisted by a college of five men called *Hosioi*, who were elected for life and chosen from a family said to have descended from Deukalion, the Greek Noah.

The Hosioi had special functions connected with the preliminary sacrifices and the preparation for the consultation. No doubt there were many other officials to act as a secretariat, keeping the records and attending to the business of the oracular service, but they did not take any part in the religious ceremonies. These were the duty of the assistant priests and novices who lived in the sanctuary. Euripides in his play *Ion* describes the work of a young priest:

> Now I will sweep the temple—
> My duty here since childhood—
> With a broom of laurel-branches,
> And purify the entrance
> With holy wreathes of flowers;
> Sprinkle the floor with water;
> And with my bow and arrows
> I'll send the wild birds flying
> That foul the temple treasures.
> Now with pure hands knowing no carnal touch
> From golden jars I sprinkle earth's pure dew
> Fresh from the swirling fountain of Castalia.[1]

Before going up to the temple, the excited inquirers would purify themselves by washing in the water of the same Kastalian Spring, then walk up the sacred way, past the statues and monuments, and past the great altar where the fires burned.

The order in which they were admitted would already have been decided. In the case of certain important visitors special priority was given, which had been established by long custom; all the others were chosen by lot.

While the visitor, who wished to consult the oracle, lodged in the city of Delphi, his life was pleasant, especially at festival times, but always there was with him the knowledge that the day was coming when he would have to go to the temple, in the very presence of the god, to put his question and receive an

[1] Euripides. *Ion. Medea and Other Plays.* Translated by Philip Vellacott, 1954.

answer. Even today, to a sensitive visitor, Delphi can seem full of the secret force of unknown powers, and to a devout pagan to whom the gods were real and terrible, the entry to the temple, only permissible after purification, would be a moment of awe and fear.

In pagan days, services were not held inside temples, as they are in churches of today; the ceremonies and sacrifices took place outside in the *temenos*, or sacred area. The temple was the home of the god himself, and its strength and beauty were all for his glory. When the god was there, only his invisible presence was felt. The gods were so awful in their might that for a mortal to see one in his real form meant instant death in a flash of consuming fire.

Inside the temple a fire of pine and laurel was kept burning continuously, which would cast flickering light on the golden armour and accoutrements belonging to the god, and at one side near the centre was the holiest place of all. This was the *adyton*, the place of the oracle. It was a small chamber below the level of the temple floor, only about eight by twelve feet square. There were two levels, the upper one having seats where the consultant sat to await the coming of the Pythia.

The Pythia was the priestess herself, the vehicle through which the god spoke. In legend, the first priestess was Phemonoe and she was also the first to give oracles in hexameter verse: the verse of Homer. At the time of Plutarch the Pythia was a peasant woman. He says:

This is the Pythia who performs the actual duty of the communication with the god. She must come from one of the most honest and respectable families who live near by and must have always lived an irreproachable life. When she descends into the place of prophecy, she does not take with her any kind of skill or talent, as she was brought up in the house of poor peasants.[1]

Even when the Pythia was a more important person, as she sometimes was in other days, it was always made clear that she had no special qualifications or education for her position. It was the god alone who spoke through her. She was not the same as a Sibyl, a seer, who possessed a special power of telling the future. There were a number of famous Sibyls who prophesied

[1] Plutarch. *Moralia*, On the Pythian Responses.

in those days, and the title has often been confused with the Pythia.

When she was chosen for her part in the oracle, the Pythia took a vow of chastity and lived in a special house in the sanctuary. In early days it was said that the Pythia was a young virgin, but later she was an older woman. Diodorus tells the story of how this came about:

It is told that Echecrates the Thessalian was present at a consultation and on looking at the virgin who gave the prophecies, he fell violently in love with her, because of her great beauty; he seized her and violated her. The Delphians as a result of this scandal decreed that in future the prophetess should not be a virgin but a woman more than fifty years old.[1]

Before the consultation with the god, the Pythia underwent a purification ceremony, and the most important part of this was the ritual bathing in the Kastalian Spring. The young priest of Euripides says:

> Servant of Delphian Apollo!
> Go to the Castalian Spring;
> Wash in its silvery eddies,
> And return cleansed to the temple
> Guard your lips from offence,
> To those who ask for oracles
> Let the god's answer come
> Pure from all private fault.[2]

This spring was also used by visitors to Delphi for purification purposes, and the Kastalian gorge may have been the lair of the Python, who lived here before Apollo came. The Pythia afterwards drank from a much more sacred spring, the Kassotis. According to Pausanias, the Kassotis flowed into a basin just above the temple, and was enclosed by a wall with a gate in it. He was also told that it flowed underground into the *adyton* of the temple, but this may have been a local guide's story, as no one else mentions it, and no trace has been found in the temple. Another important spring in those days was the Delphousa

[1] Diodorus Siculus. *World History*: XVI.
[2] Euripides. *Ion*.

which rises higher up the slope and provides the modern village of Delphi with its water supply.

After her preparation the Pythia entered the temple in simple white robes, and accompanied by the prophet, descended into the *adyton*.

The anxious inquirers had already been conducted to their places: 'I will take you to the sanctuary door; inside you will be guided by others, Delphian noblemen, appointed by lot to places near the Tripod Throne,'[1] the young priest Ion says.

The visitors would hear the murmur of voices and occasionally they would smell a strange perfume. This is one of the mysterious happenings described by Plutarch. The odour varied in intensity, sometimes it was faint and at other times it came in great strength, and smelt 'like the sweetest and most precious of perfumes'. Some accounts say that the priest burned barley and chopped bay leaves sprinkled with hemp, and that the Pythia chewed laurel leaves in order to produce the state of trance in which she spoke her prophecies. The smoke of the burning offerings would fill the *adyton* with choking fumes, some of which, in escaping, would be smelt by the postulants in the room above. Plutarch, however, did not describe the perfume in this way, and he, at least, knew what was going on in the secret chamber. The chewing of laurel leaves and the fumigation would more likely have made the Pythia feel sick, and is not a very satisfactory form of producing inspiration. If they were used at all, they were part of the purification ceremony. The solemn surroundings, the music and the rites, together with the knowledge of the presence of the god would all be sufficient to produce 'ecstasy'. Trances and states of possession are still to be found among some people today, produced by far less stimulation than there was at Delphi. In Plutarch's time they regarded the perfume as a psychic manifestation and part of the deep mystery of how the god inspired the Pythia. The frenzy and wild hysteria of the Pythia, so popular in later accounts, do not seem to agree with the representations of her on pottery and in sculpture, where she has a calm and ecstatic beauty, at least when the consultation was successful, and when Plutarch describes her voice as being soft and musical.

[1] Euripides. *Ion.*

The fantasies of a demented Pythia, intoxicated by the poisonous fumes, or physically impregnated by the god in an atmosphere of terror and darkness were probably quite false. The whole ceremony in the temple was most likely quite simple and very much more moving. The Pythia, as we know, was a respectable woman, the daughter of a poor farmer. After bathing in the waters of Kastalia and drinking from the Kassotis, she put on her simple white robes and was led past the waiting people, to the small enclosed cell. Here she would sit near the statue of Apollo—a beautiful young god—looking down on her with grave, understanding eyes. In one hand she would take the woollen cord; the cord which linked her with the holy *omphalos*, and with the other hand she would hold the branch of laurel.

Soon the laurel leaves would shake and the Pythia would go quietly into 'ecstasy', that gentle trance which was in its true sense ecstatic, for she was possessed by the god. There would be the smell of incense, and music would be heard. It is unimaginable that Apollo, the god of music, would not be greeted by singing and the sound of flutes or harps.

The Pythia would start to speak and the prophet would record her words. Later she would recover, remembering little perhaps, of what she had said, and return to her quiet duties about the temple.

We shall never really know what took place, in spite of many hundreds of years of speculation, but throughout history there have been girls who have heard the voices of angels.

After the Pythia had spoken her message, in whatever way the words came or were inspired, the prophet returned to the waiting postulant with the answer to the inquiry.

It was never made quite clear whether the Pythia actually spoke plainly in prose or verse, or whether the prophet had to make what sense he could from her incoherent words. It was suggested that the god himself produced the oracular message, but in any case it was often very difficult to understand. The prophet and his staff had to make it partly intelligible at least and even then there was at hand an official called an exegete to explain the general sense. There have been some cynical suggestions that at times the prophet instructed the Pythia as to what she should say. More faithful believers thought that Apollo protected his priests by being careful to adjust the responses so as not to bring the Delphians into peril, when they were so often at a disadvantage.

The prophet dictated the reply of the Pythia to the inquiry and, on request, it was put into writing. Very important oracles were often engraved on stone as a permanent record.

If the inquirer was a courier who had come from one of the city states with a written question, the reply was given to him in a sealed tablet, which he was under solemn oath not to open.

Sometimes the oracles were simple statements in prose and at other times they were given in verse form. There are records of oracles in which both forms are used. One version was a straightforward prose response and there was a formal, poetic reply for publication. The presentation of an oracle varied with the importance of the occasion and the use of verse waxed and waned with the prestige of Delphi. Verse oracles were hardly known at all between 100 B.C. and A.D. 100, when the importance of Delphi was at a low ebb.

The variations of the oracle seem to be a measure of the enthusiasm and diligence of the priests, and the prophet and his staff must have had a great deal to do with the versification of the responses.

The inquirers were never allowed to question the oracle or to cross-examine the god in historical times, but it was possible to ask a supplementary question if the first answer was not sufficiently clear. Sometimes they would ask for advice from friends in Delphi, about the putting of further questions, as the Athenian delegates did at the time of the Persian invasion. 'Timon, the son of Androbulus, a man reputed at Delphi equally with the best, advised them to take supplicatory branches and to go again and consult the oracle as supplicants.'[1]

In later historical times the methods and formulae of the consultation were firmly fixed, and it was only in legendary days— the time of the Greek colonization and the growth of Delphi, that the Pythia answered the unspoken question of the inquirer immediately he entered the temple, which happened on some occasions.

The oracular service at Delphi was part of the established order of things, and all that was necessary was to approach it

[1] Herodotus. *History*: VII. 141. Translated by Henry Cary, 1847.

in a reverent spirit, to frame your question with care, and to observe the regulations. Divination at other places was a doubtful business and chance played its part. At Delphi it was not a question of chance, it was a glimpse of truth given by a god, even if the answer was misunderstood, or sometimes wrongly interpreted.

4 · 'Omphalos', Tripod and Laurel

PLUTARCH said that three things were essential to the oracle; the water of the sacred springs, the tripod and the laurel. It is doubtful if the water of Kassotis actually flowed through the *adyton*, but it was certainly part of the preparation of the Pythia, and the Kastalian Spring, once only regarded as a source of purification, became exalted in later years, and was thought to be the true fount of inspiration. There was a golden, or gilded statue of Apollo in the holy place, together with the *omphalos*, branches of laurel and a mysterious chasm. The *omphalos*, tripod and laurel are shown in one form or another in numerous pictures and carvings, and there is no doubt that they existed. The chasm from which the sacred emanations came is a much more doubtful matter. Although it has long been part of story and legend, its real use may have been symbolic rather than actual. It was not difficult to believe that in some strange way a crack opened in the earth—invisible to mortal eyes—through which a mysterious vapour rose.

Whether or not the emanation was a mystical one, there was never any real mystery intended about the oracle at Delphi. At Eleusis, thousands of initiates year after year kept their secret so well that hardly any mention has ever been made of what took place. The people who were being prepared for initiation were known as *mystai*, and it therefore became a true mystery cult. At Delphi, on the contrary, so much was written and there was so much discussion about the oracle, that the spate of words in itself has led to endless disputes among scholars. As the oracle was so well known, nobody unfortunately wrote a very clear account of the procedure, thinking perhaps it was not necessary. On the other hand the romantic fame of the oracle was so great that poets and philosophers wrote at length and with vivid imagination, often without ever having visited Delphi.

The Romans in particular found the oracle a wonderful subject, and legends grew more and more contradictory. Lucan, the

poet who lived in the time of Nero, wrote exaggerated verse
and tells the story of how Appius consulted the Delphic
Oracle. At that time, a hundred years before Lucan, the oracle
had been closed to the public for a long time. He says it was
because Pyrrhus, King of Epirus, was afraid to hear the truth
about the future, and had ordered it to be silent. When Appius
came to consult the oracle he demanded that it should be re-
opened for him. He dragged the 'Pythoness' towards the shrine
and pushed the terrified woman inside. She was afraid to enter
the innermost sanctuary and made many excuses. 'The priest
tied one laurel wreath, bound with white wool, above her brows
in the form of a fillet and used another to secure the long tresses
behind,' and she pretended to be possessed. This did not fool
Appius, who shouted at her: 'You impious creature, I have
come to enquire about the fate of this distracted world. Unless
you stop speaking in your natural voice and go down to the
chasm for true inspiration, the gods whose oracles you are taking
in vain will punish you—and so will I!'

The girl was terrified, so she:

. . . approached the lip of the chasm and seated herself on the tripod. . . .
Apollo genuinely possessed her at last. He forced his way into her
heart, masterful as ever, driving out her private thoughts and draining
her body of all that was mortal, so that he could possess it wholly. She
went blundering frantically about the shrine, with the god mounted
on the nape of her neck, knocking over the tripods that stood in her
path. The hair rose on her scalp and when she tossed her head the
wreaths went flying across the bare floor.

Lucan continues in the same vein for a long time, describing
the frenzy of the girl with a mixture of eloquence and comic
melodrama until . . . 'The priestess ran full tilt against the
Temple doors, broke them open and rushed out. She was still in
ecstacy, not having been able to expel the god.'[1] Eventually 'the
spirit of divine truth departed and returned whence it had
come,' and the priestess was revived with difficulty.

Lucan's vivid story might possibly have given us a clue as to
what happened, but for the fact that, apparently, there was no
chasm in the earth at the site of Apollo's temple. The idea of

[1] Lucan. *Pharsalia*. Translated by Robert Graves, 1956.

chasms and vents through which vapours arose from the under-world was very familiar to the Romans. Lucan described the working of the oracle as by means of an essence that seeped up from a chasm.

There the priestess inhales it, and when it reaches her heart she bellows forth prophecies for all to hear; very much as the flames in the centre of Etna send lava boiling over its lip. . . . Every honest visitant may approach this holy spot, but it must never be defiled by criminals. Moreover, no wicked requests are whispered here, since prayer is banned—the god merely announces irrevocable doom.[1]

Strabo, in the first century B.C. wrote: 'They say that the Oracle is a hollow perpendicular cavern, with a not very large mouth. Out of this rises an air which causes frenzy, and above the mouth there is placed a lofty tripod upon which the Pythia mounts and inhaling the air prophesies.'[2]

Descriptions of this kind coloured the stories of the oracle for many years, especially after the oracle had ceased to function. Even Christian writers carried on the tradition of imaginative stories based on earlier accounts. In order to discredit the pagan beliefs, and entertain their followers, they included indecent suggestions about the physical impregnation of the Pythia as she sat on the tripod.

The principal source of modern theories about the working of the oracle is the writing of Plutarch who was an intelligent and observant man, and as a high priest of the temple was in a position to know the facts. But even he left enough unsolved problems to cause arguments among later classical scholars.

The idea of a physical fissure in the earth from which an emanation arose, has been disposed of by archaeologists who can find no trace of such a thing. It was suggested that the fissure had been closed by an earthquake and Lucan himself said that it may have been filled by sand from the destruction of the temple by the Gauls, but the geological nature of the rock makes this extremely improbable. In spite of this the tradition of the fissure lasted many centuries.

There were not only legends about a narrow fissure, but also

[1] Lucan. *Pharsalia.*
[2] Strabo. *Geographies*: 9. 3. 5. Translated by H. C. Jones, 1924.

even more ancient stories about an oracular cave. Byron, in his note on Delphi before there were any excavations, says: 'A little above Castri is a cave supposed the Pythian, of immense depth, the upper part of it is paved and now a cowhouse,'[1] but no trace of such a cave has been discovered. The original myths of Delphi refer to a cave beneath the mountain, and the oracle of Earth should have some sort of cave as its source. Joseph Fontenrose, American professor of classics at the University of California, has been interested in the oracle at Delphi for over twenty years, and suggests that the original oracle was to be found in the Korykian cave.[2]

This cave is on the steep slope of a hill five hundred feet above the Parnassian plateau, 2,600 feet above Delphi, and seven miles away. The hill is now known as Sarandavli, meaning 'forty courts'. You reach it from Delphi by means of a steep stony track, known to the ancients as the 'bad stair'. The Korykian cave is well known as a place of refuge to the people of Delphi, during times of war and invasion, but it has also been the haunt of outlaws and bandits. It is difficult of access and invisible from below, but from the ledge in front of the entrance can be seen a vast panorama of the slopes of Parnassos and no enemy could approach it unobserved. The cave is very dark and deep and it is not a pleasant place in which to live. The dripping water which forms stalagmites and stalagtites makes the steep floor slimy and dangerous, but it was very much admired in ancient times. Inscriptions show that like most caves in Greece, it was important to Pan and the nymphs, as well as to Apollo and Dionysos.

Strabo said that the Delphians originally lived higher up the mountain at a small town called Lykorea, not far from Delphi. Some time before 800 B.C. they moved down the mountainside to live at the site known later as Pytho.

It has always been a problem to account for the lack of a cave or fissure in Delphi itself, but geologists have quite firmly stressed its impossibility on that site. The Korykian cave would account for all the memories of an oracular chasm and fit very well with the myths of Apollo as they were told. The explanation given of artificial cracks and fissures in the *adyton* of the

[1] Byron. Note to *Childe Harold*: Canto I. 1.
[2] Joseph Fontenrose. *Python*, 1959.

temple or the suggestions that toxic vapours were produced by the priests can all be shown as misrepresentations of the true facts.

Professor Fontenrose compares the Korykian cave with a cave near Korykos in Cicilia from whence the worship of Apollo is thought to have come. It seems to me that the name *Delphi* might be a yet older name for the cave, and from it the people of Lykorea would have been known as Delphians. Delphis, the name which was used in the time of Plato, is an old word for 'womb', and by the stone-age hunter, a cave was often regarded as a 'magic womb in which the fertility totem was maintained'. The earliest cult was that of Mother Earth, and a cave of this kind would have been an obvious site for her worship. In the cave was, perhaps, the fetish stone, the *omphalos*, which the Delphians venerated so much.

In the temple of Apollo, the most sacred object and the most ancient, was the *omphalos*. It was the marking stone of the world's navel, or centre, and occupied an important place in the *adyton*. By its means the Pythia was induced to speak. When she was in contact with it she was in contact with the hidden powers of the earth, and the force stored in this small stone flowed through her, leaving her prepared to accept the coming of the god himself. In some legends, the *omphalos* was said to be the navel cord of Zeus, which fell off in Crete, but the eighth-century Greek poet Hesiod says that the *omphalos* in Delphi was the original stone swallowed by Kronos.

Kronos was the god who ruled the world before the coming of new and more glorious deities, his children, the Olympian gods. He was afraid that they would become mightier than he and overthrow him, as they later did, so he thought of an unpleasant way of dealing with the problem: by eating his children as soon as they were born. His wife, Rhea, naturally objected to this, so when she gave birth to Zeus, she hid the child, and gave the mighty Kronos a stone wrapped in swaddling clothes to swallow. Later, when Kronos was overcome by Zeus, he disgorged all the children he had previously swallowed. Hesiod says:

> The stone he first disgorged,
> He last devoured.
> This Jove on widely traversable earth

> Fixed in bless'd Pythos, underneath the chasm
> Of cleft Parnassos, to succeeding times a
> monument and miracle to men.[1]

Pausanias says that this stone, referred to by Hesiod, is not the true *omphalos*, but one which lay outside the temple in the enclosure and that priestesses anointed it with oil every day and put raw wool on it at festival times.

According to Professor Cook, the early Greeks, like many people, thought the earth was flat with a central boss, which was the *omphalos*, and that the *omphalos* was originally a mound of earth with a central pillar which supported the sky. Pillars were often used as symbols of worship, and the image of Apollo was sometimes poetically referred to as a lofty pillar.

The connection between the *omphalos* and the pillar is doubtful and it was certainly never shown in the many representations in ancient art. The function and shape of the *omphalos* has other significances, as we shall see, reflected in the rites of Dionysos.

Near the entrance to the museum at Delphi, is a large egg-shaped marble stone which is a copy of the *omphalos*. It stood on the terrace outside the temple for visitors to admire, and Pausanias remarked on it when he was there in the second century A.D. The real stone, the holiest object of all, was of course, in the *adyton*, where the general public could not see it. On the replica is carved a representation of the net of knotted woollen strands which covered the true *omphalos* and was in some way connected with the ritual use of the stone by the Pythia.

On each side of the *omphalos* in the *adyton* stood a solid golden eagle in commemoration of the finding of the centre of the earth by the eagles of Zeus. The sanctity of the stone, however, did not prevent the Phokians from melting down the eagles when they were in need of war funds. They had to be replaced later out of the fine that was imposed on the Phokians when they were defeated.

In September 1913 a small stone, about a foot high, was discovered in the temple excavations by F. Courby, and archaeologists all over the world were impressed by this discovery of the true *omphalos*. This strange stone was for some time placed on

[1] Hesiod. *Theogony*: 596. Translated by C. A. Elton.

top of the replica of the *omphalos* in the museum. It is a rough limestone block, with a square hole through the centre. From the hole projects a piece of iron like a knife blade, which is wedged in by two nails. The most exciting part of the find was in what appeared to be letters carved on the stone. These were interpreted as meaning 'of earth' and there was also the magic letter 'E' which was connected with the temple at Delphi in some mystic way that has never been wholly explained.

The find was described as 'among the most brilliant archaeological discoveries of our time'; but alas for the short-lived fame of archaeologists and the difficulties that surround a profession which is not unlike a detective story in its continued seeking for clues. The stone discovered by Courby is now believed to be the cupola of a wayside shrine. Even more deflating to the triumphal announcement over fifty years ago, is the announcement by Professor Bousquet that the metal blade in Courby's stone has an inscription on it that can with certainty be dated about A.D. 1860.

The search for the true *omphalos* goes on and there are several contenders for the honour amongst the stones that lie in the grass by the excavations. Stones which may be seen and touched by unsuspecting visitors today.

Apart from the *omphalos*, the other indispensable item in the *adyton* was the tripod. The Pythian tripod shown in so many pictures had three straight, upright legs, supporting a deep bowl or cauldron, not unlike a font. The edge of the bowl was often ornamented with large upright handles, in the form of rings or circles.

The tripod was a sacred symbol, and it probably once had a magical significance as well as a practical purpose. Early man quickly realized that a three-legged structure was the simplest rigid support, whatever the length of individual legs, and they may have seen this as another mysterious attribute of the magic number three. The tripod, traditionally, was connected with Delphi and the love of order and balance which was one of the blessings brought to men by Apollo. Pious and grateful benefactors presented tripods of all shapes and sizes to the temple. From various accounts, it seems that large numbers of them were erected in the temple area, and some of them have been found by archaeologists. The tripod was also used in monuments and was a favoured shape to commemorate the winners of the Pythian Games, held in Delphi.

Many accounts refer to the Pythia sitting on the tripod, but it seems to have been a difficult and uncomfortable seat. In some pictures of the scene, the god Apollo is shown seated on the tripod and the priestess is shown standing near by. There does seem to be a possibility that the Pythia did not actually sit on the holy tripod, which was reserved for the god, but sat near it. The Ashanti tribe in West Africa, have a sacred stool which is venerated and carried in processions with an umbrella over it, but no one is allowed to sit on it, as it is regarded as the seat of the god of the tribe. In the same way the tripod in the *adyton* may have been the seat of Apollo only. On the other hand, if the Pythia really identified herself with the god and was possessed by him, she might have sat in the bowl of the tripod.

It has been suggested that the Pythia sat on a three-legged chair, an influence which came from Mycenean days when thrones often had three legs, as is indicated by the terra-cotta models of thrones found among Mycenaean remains. In Roman times the tripod at Delphi was often referred to as a table, and the *mensa delphica* was the familiar name given to many three-legged tables in Italy.

In any event the tripod had magical powers and Plutatch described the violent effect on the Pythia when she touched it as similar to falling in love.

Professor A. B. Cook suggests that if the Pythia, a mere mortal, is raised to the status of a goddess by her connection with Apollo, then she must undergo a ritual to mark this change. He points out that in many myths and folk stories this change was brought about by boiling the person concerned, whereupon mortality and old age falls away leaving perpetual youth. In very ancient times the dead were boiled to remove the flesh from their bones in order to liberate the soul. Professor Cook suggests that the Pythia underwent some sort of make-believe, ritual boiling in the pot at the top of the tripod.[1]

It was believed by the Romans that the bones and teeth of the python who originally guarded the oracle, were kept in the tripod, and this is also mentioned in the Dionysian stories.

In some ways, it seems that the French, who have spent over

[1] A. B. Cook. *Zeus*, Vol. II, 1925.

a hundred years excavating Delphi, and have a special sympathy with Apollo as the god of reason, were not very happy about all the supernatural implications of the oracle. Pierre Amandry, the French scholar, recently suggested a more matter-of-fact approach to the use of the tripod and to the whole oracle itself.[1] He favours the idea that the oracle was given in the form of a lottery. It was suggested by Professor Holland and others that the bowl of the tripod contained lots, or pebbles, and that these in themselves were regarded as sacred relics—perhaps even the bones and teeth of the python, or of Dionysos.

There is evidence that on occasions the Pythia shook the tripod, or it shook of its own accord when questions were put to it. This may have been part of the magical rite concerned with the passing of its divine power to the Pythia, but Amandry believes that the shaking of the tripod was the natural action that someone would make before drawing lots from it. He quotes Roulez who, in 1867, said that the lots had markings on them, and when one was drawn or made to jump out of the vessel the Pythia, after interpreting the significance of the symbols, pronounced her divine answer. This, of course, is very similar to other methods of divination, in which bones are thrown to the ground and answers given according to their positions.

In many pictures the Pythia is shown holding a shallow bowl, which might refer to the drawing of lots from it, as Amandry suggests, or perhaps, as is more usually believed, she may be seeking inspiration by looking into it. Messelière says that both methods may have been used at one time or another according to the type of question asked, but what did it matter if the god was there?

What power influenced the throw of the dice, or turned the marked slip of bone to yes or no, or revealed the black or white bean? What was it that moved the hand of the Pythia as she shook the urn, as great questions were posed at the tripod? Away from Delphi it was luck, but at Delphi it was a god. The god who had promised never to deceive those who, having observed the sacred rites, could come to him with confidence.[2]

[1] Pierre Amandry. *La Mantique Apollienne à Delphes*, 1950.
[2] P. de la Cost-Messelière. *Delphes*.

The last of the great forces of the oracle was the laurel. The laurel has always been associated with rites and festivals at Delphi from its earliest myth. As Euripides describes the Python at Delphi, it is reminiscent of the scene in the Garden of Eden:

> And there, behold, an ancient Snake
> Wine-eyed, bronze-gleaming in the brake
> Of deep-leaved laurel, ruled the dell,
> Sent by old Earth from under
> Strange eaves to guard her Oracle—
> A thing of fear and wonder.[1]

Wreaths of laurel garlanded the winners of the Pythian contests. The laurel wreath given, in fancy or metaphor, to the poet or musician today, has been handed down from the Pythian Apollo, but we do not often think of the wreathes of olive or parsley equally honoured by the victors in other parts of ancient Greece.[2] The laurel was used as a symbol for Delphi: in pictures it twined round the tripod and crowned Apollo; its branches were carried by the Pythia and even the consultants. Before she entered the *adyton* the Pythia was fumigated by the smoke of burning laurel and she may even have chewed a little of it. Most important of all, she shook a branch of laurel at the moment of revelation. It was also believed that the oracle may once have been heard in the sound of the wind in the leaves of laurel trees, and though such inefficient methods were no longer needed by Apollo, some memory of it remained. Plutarch speaks of the perpetual fire in the temple where only pine logs were burnt, but on which laurel leaves were thrown in place of incense, and laurel would no doubt be burning on the great altar outside the temple.

We do not know why the laurel was so important but, like the holly, it is an evergreen, the symbol of life during dark winter days.

Whatever happened in the *adyton*, whether the Pythia was

[1] Euripides. *Iphigenia in Tauris*: V, 1,245 *et seq*. Translated by Gilbert Murray, 1910.
[2] Olympic games: wild olive. Nemean games: wild parsley. Isthmian games: wild parsley or pine. Only at the Pythian games were laurel wreaths awarded.

truly possessed and spoke, or whether she drew lots from a tripod bowl, the faith in the power of the old cult objects, real or symbolic, was sufficient to make her respond to the inspiration of the god. We do not know clearly how it was done, but it worked well enough to influence and help many generations of men.

5 · *Apollo*

IT was the fame of the oracle that brought wealth to Delphi. Sometimes gifts were given out of gratitude for the help the oracle had provided, but at other times they were sent with a hope that the oracle could be persuaded to give a favourable reply to a question. Whether or not the oracle could be bribed, it was certain that the very human priests could be influenced by the generosity of the consultants, and the gold and silver that was showered on Delphi was talked of in the farthest parts of the barbarian world. It was little wonder that when marauding tribes descended on Greece to loot and plunder, it was to the famous Delphi that their first steps were turned.

The material wealth was undoubtedly due to the oracle, but the wealth of beauty, the dedication of the finest works of art was not for an oracle but for a god. Delphi was not the home of a local deity, but the centre, political as well as religious, of a faith which was essentially Greek. It was the sanctuary of a powerful and sometimes terrible god, but a god found worthy of love and respect by the greatest men of their times, and it was here that he was worshipped. This god was known as Phoebus the 'shining one', Musagetes the 'leader of the muses' and even Loxias the 'devious', when his oracles were particularly obscure, and by many other names; but the most famous of these was Apollo. As Apollo he was worshipped by Greeks and Romans alike. He was the only Olympian god whose name was not changed eventually from Greek to Latin.

In one of the oldest hymns to Apollo sung in 700 B.C., it was obvious that to the Greeks he was the greatest of all the gods next to Zeus. All the other gods feared him and gave way before him, except for his gentle mother, Leto. The old hymn said:

I will remember and not be unmindful of Apollo, who shoots from afar. As he goes through the house of Zeus the gods tremble before him and all spring up from their seats when he draws near, as

51

he bends his bright bow. But Leto alone stays by the side of Zeus who delights in thunder, and then she unstrings his bow, and closes his quiver, and takes his archery from his strong shoulders in her hands and hangs them on a golden peg against a pillar of his father's house. Then she leads him to a seat and makes him sit: and the father gives him nectar in a golden cup welcoming his dear son, while the other gods sit down there, and queenly Leto rejoices that she bore a mighty son and an archer.[1]

The Romans never found an easy substitute for Apollo in their approach to the Olympian gods, and wherever his influence spread, something of the Greek spirit went with it.

Apollo was the god of light, order and reason; and also of healing, but he could be deadly too. The arrows he carried were like the sun, which at midday can strike a man down. They were shafts of reason and clear-thinking which could shatter illusion, and destroy the self-satisfied complacency of men. At the same time he was the god of music and song. Under his rule the poets and singers and artists were allied with the scientists and politicians. The Greeks, through their worship of Apollo, made a special contribution to the life of the ancient world. To the followers of Apollo, the imagination and insight of poetic vision, the love and recognition of beauty was combined with a self-discipline that the true artist recognizes as the one means of realizing and making concrete his ideas. The search for forms of good government, or the study of the natural world were undertaken in his name as means of increasing man's harmony with his world or of revealing its order and beauty.

A hymn of Kallimachos, the chief librarian of the famous library in Alexandria, reveals how deeply he was regarded by his followers in the third century B.C.

Golden is the tunic of Apollo and golden his mantle, his lyre and his Lycian bow and his quiver: golden too are his sandals; for rich in gold is Apollo, rich also in possessions; by Pytho might thou guess, and ever beautiful is he and ever young; never on the girl cheeks of Apollo have come so much as the down of manhood. His locks distil fragrant oil upon the ground; not oil of fat do the locks of Apollo distil but very Healing of all. And in whatsoever city do those dews fall upon the ground, in that city all things are free from harm. To him belongs

[1] *Hesiod and Homeric Hymns.* Translated by H. G. Evelyn-White, 1914.

the archer, to him the minstrel. His are the lots of diviner and, his seers; from Phoebus the physicians have learned the art of delaying death. And Phoebus it is that men follow when they map out cities, and Phoebus himself doth weave their foundations![1]

For a short time during the fifth century B.C. in Athens, under the influence of the young gods Apollo and Athene, there was a triumphant vindication of the Greek spirit, but the jealousies and quarrels between one Greek and another were reflected in a decline in values. There came an age of doubt and cynicism, when the old Olympian gods of Homer were often discredited by thinkers and playwrights. In those days they turned more and more to Apollo as the one god worthy of veneration.

Euripides, described by Aristotle as 'the most tragic of the poets', was the last of the great dramatists of classical Greece. He often wrote in despair over the fate of doomed mankind, but his choruses all spoke of the Delphic appeal to moderation as the only escape from the violence of men's passions, and, among the gods, only Apollo showed any real concern for man's condition.

Socrates, who was called the wisest of men by the Delphic Oracle, and his pupil Plato only truly respected Apollo among the pantheon of gods. In this they were following the thinking of earlier philosophers, such as Heraklitus, who taught that the essence of the universe was change, and who was a follower of Apollo, and of course there was the great Pythagoras, whose name suggests a connection with the Pythia.

Pythagoras died about 500 B.C. and, although little is known about him as a person, he founded a school, or brotherhood, known as the Pythagorean, which had as its rule the teaching of the greatness of the worship of Pythian Apollo in all its aspects. As every schoolboy knows, the Pythagoreans developed the art of mathematics. Although they may not have invented Pythagoras' theorem, they went further and saw the rule of number as the foundation of the universe. The music of Apollo's lyre was first analysed by the Pythagoreans when the length of a string was found to determine the pitch of a note. It was a revelation to them that a note, an octave higher than another, is produced by a string of exactly half the length.

[1] *Callimachus*. Translated by A. W. Mair, 1921.

E

The discovery of the mathematical proportions existing in music led them to conclude that the whole universe followed a musical and mathematical pattern. It has since been shown that musical ratios are physiological phenomena depending on the structure of the ear alone. Sir James Jeans pointed this out in 1937,[1] but in the light of modern scientific knowledge he also concluded that 'the Great Architect of the Universe now begins to appear as a pure mathematician',[2] a conclusion with which the Pythagoreans would have heartily agreed.

The Pythagorean philosophy went far deeper than mathematical research and had profound influence on thinkers for many generations. They had a passionate devotion to the idea of form and law. They believed that the order of the universe, the *kosmos*, when understood by men could be imitated, bringing a similar order known as *kosmios* to men's souls. Partly because of a belief in the transmigration of souls they were vegetarians and it was said that it was only on Delos, the birth-place of Apollo, that Pythagoras would worship, as here no animal sacrifices were permitted on the strange altar built by Apollo from the left side horns of animals. It was a contemporary of Pythagoras, the poet Xenophanes, who satyrized his belief in transmigration, by the story of a man beating a dog. A passer-by called out: 'Stop, don't beat him! It's the soul of a friend of mine, I recognize his voice.'

To thinkers and philosophers, Apollo at Delphi signified the profound principle of man's aspirations towards light and reason, away from the dark forces of materialism, but like the other Olympian gods, there were familiar myths and stories told about him and his deeds. These were sung as hymns or told as story and legend by countless ordinary worshippers. Some of these were ancient and spoke of the origins of the worship of the god, and some were allegories reflecting his qualities.

Among Greeks, the stories about the gods were not fixed in the form of a litany or sacred book. Story-tellers and poets enlarged on the old tales to the delight of their audiences, often with humour and bawdy wit. Although the gods were feared and sacrilege could produce the utmost disaster, and there were moments of terror in their worship hard to imagine today, they

[1] Sir James Jeans. *Science and Music*, 1937.
[2] Sir James Jeans. *The Mysterious Universe*, 1930.

were paradoxically so familiar that comic poets joked about them without any sense of blasphemy.

Serious philosophers like Plato protested about the telling of frivolous stories, in particular the stories about the cruelty and fallibility of the gods, especially to children. He wrote: 'Children cannot distinguish between what is allegory and what isn't, and opinions formed at that age are usually difficult to eradicate or change.' Certainly it was the role of poets to tell stories about the gods, but it was their duty to present a truthful picture:

God must surely always be represented as he is, whether the poet is writing epic, lyric or drama. . . . The truth is that God is good, and he must be so described.

> But nothing good is harmful or can do harm.
> And what does no harm does no evil.
> Nor can a thing which does no evil be the cause of evil. . . .

Then of our laws laying down the principle which those who write or speak about the gods must follow, one should be this—God is the source of good only.[1]

Although some of the stories about the gods were unworthy of the religious truths Plato felt should be expressed, some of the most beautiful poetry and the loveliest art the world has ever known has been created under their influence, and it is only natural that for Apollo, who was the god of poetry and beauty, some of the most lyrical verses should be written.

All the stories and songs about Apollo suggest that he was not originally worshipped at Delphi. As Professor Guthrie points out, the name Apollo is not Hellenic in origin; he says: 'At Delphi he was remembered by the Greeks themselves as a late-comer, who had succeeded generations of earlier tenants to the shrine.'[2]

According to the old hymns, he was born on Delos, a small island near Mykonos, in the Aegean. It is the centre of the group of islands known as the Kyklades—the circular ones—and from it across the blue sea can be seen, far away, the mountain peaks of the guarding islands which surround it on every side. Even today it has an unsubstantial, dream-like quality and

[1] Plato. *The Republic*: Part 3, Book 2. Translated by H. D. P. Lee, 1955.
[2] W. K. C. Guthrie. *The Greeks and their Gods.*

once it was believed to have floated without foundation. The oldest hymn of Apollo, said: 'For of old time it drifted about before the waves and stress of winds from every side.'[1] Kallimachos wrote many years later: 'There is to be seen in the waters a tiny island wandering over the seas. Her feet abide not in one place, but on the tide she swims even as a stalk of asphodel, where the south wind blows, whithersoever the sea carries her.'[2]

As Delphi was the holiest site on the mainland of Greece, so was Delos the holiest of all the islands of the Mediterranean Sea.

The Delian hymns told the story of Leto, the mother of Apollo . . .

> Robed with azure, ever mild;
> Placid to men and to immortal gods;
> Mild from the first beginning of her days;
> Gentlest of all in heaven.[3]

Leto was loved by Zeus and when she conceived, Hera, the wife of Zeus, was bitterly jealous and determined to make the birth as difficult as possible.

Far roamed Leto in travail with the god who shoots afar, to see if any land would be willing to make a dwelling for her son. But they greatly trembled and feared [the wrath of Hera] and none, not even the richest of them, dared receive Phoibus, until queenly Leto set foot on Delos and uttered winged words and asked the isle: 'Delos, would you be willing to be the abode of my son Apollo and make him a rich temple? For no other will touch you, as you will find: and I think you will never be rich in oxen and sheep nor bear vintage nor yet produce plants abundantly. But if you have the temple of far-shooting Apollo, all men will bring you hecatombs and gather here, and incessant savour of rich sacrifice will always arise.'[4]

Delos consented, and: '. . . Verily from roots deep down in the earth there sprang upright four pillars with adamantine base, and on their capitals they held up the rock.'[5] When the

---

[1] Pindar. *Odes*: Fragment, in honour of Delos. Translated by E. M. Myers, 1892.
[2] Callimachus.
[3] Callimachus.
[4] *Hesiod and Homeric Hymns.*
[5] Pindar. *Odes*: Fragment.

island was firmly anchored in place, Leto bore Apollo, by the sacred lake. It was not an easy delivery and the birth pangs lasted for nine days and nine nights until at last Leto 'cast her arms about a palm tree and kneeled on a soft meadow while the earth laughed for joy beneath. Then the child leaped forth to the light, and all the godesses raised a cry. Straightway, great Phoibus, the godesses washed you purely, and cleanly with sweet water, and swathed you in a white garment of fine texture, new woven, and fastened a golden band about you.'[1]

Soon after his birth the golden baby took his bow and his arrows and set out to seek a home, from which he could reign and bring guidance to men. After looking in many places, he came to Krissos below Parnassos, and near there at Delphi he found the perfect shrine at the world's centre, a fitting home for a god. In those days, before his arrival, Delphi was guarded by a dragon, or giant snake, and the oracle was the special preserve of Themis, the daughter of Mother Earth, Ge. Apollo fought the dragon, killed it and took possession of the oracle. The chorus of Euripides' play, *Iphigenia in Tauris*, tells the story in praise of Apollo.

> Thou, Phoebus, still a new-born thing,
> Meet in thy mother's arms to lie,
> Didst kill the Snake and crown thee king,
> In Pytho's land of prophecy:
> Thine was the tripod and the chair
> Of golden truth; and throned there,
> Hard by the streams of Castaly,
> Beneath the untrodden portal
> Of Earth's mid-stone there flows from thee
> Wisdom for all things mortal.[2]

The rotting or *pythein* of the corpse of the snake gave its name to the sanctuary and the god became known as Pythian Apollo. The ancient female cult contributed to the function of the oracle in later years by the retention of a female Pythia among the male priests of Apollo.

The myth of a god fighting a dragon is a universal one, and appears in the folk-lore of every nation throughout the world. In

[1] *Hesiod and Homeric Hymns.*
[2] Euripides. *Iphigenia in Tauris.*

Delphi's neighbouring village of Arachova, St George is still the patron saint. At one time it was believed that this myth was a simple one of the conquest of light over darkness, but with the more sophisticated Freudian theories of the twentieth century it was claimed that the myth represented the conflict of Eros and Thanatos; the death-instinct and the life-instinct which are inherent in all living organisms. The most probable theory is the one accepted by many Greeks, that it represents the triumphant but continual struggle of man in his aspirations towards a nobler life of reason, which they regarded as a male as opposed to a female, earth-bound principle. There is the reservation that at Delphi it was only possible with the co-operation of a female in the person of the Pythia.

According to Euripides, Mother Earth avenged herself by producing confused dreams among the mortals who visited Delphi, until Apollo, still a baby, went to Zeus and claimed his rights to the sanctuary.

> Zeus laughed to see the babe, I trow,
> So swift to claim his golden rite;
> He laughed and bowed his head, in vow
> To still those voices of the night.
> And so from out the eyes of men
> That dark dream-truth was lost again;
> And Phoebus, throned where the throng
> Prays at the golden portal
> Again doth shed in sunlit song
> Hope unto all things mortal.[1]

The defeat of the Python did not mean the easy establishment of Apollo at Delphi, there were many struggles with jealous older gods. As Messelière says: 'The legends all spoke of discord and struggles in the origins of the Delphic sanctuary. They were fables but who can deny that they were based on reality? The centre of the world so loved by gods and men, would have been the scene of dissension and the field of battle. It is one of its most noticeable characteristics and it remained so throughout the ages.'[2]

The ancient god, Poseidon, claimed certain rites in the

[1] Euripides. *Iphigenia in Tauris.*
[2] P. de la Cost-Messelière. *Delphes.*

sanctuary and had to be propitiated. Hermes, the cunning god of thieves and merchants, claimed 'the same sacred privileges as Apollo and threatened to come to Pytho and force the vast house, and in the pillage to carry off quantities of tripods and magnificent gold cauldrons and shining arms in quantities'. Apollo conceded to Hermes the uncertain divinations, the chances of lotteries and the telling of fortunes by cards. He was forbidden to be oracle-speaking. Apollo also gave him the services of the three maiden sisters, the Thriai, who lived 'under a fold of Parnassos' and from whom Apollo had learnt many things. . . . 'They eat honeycomb and bring everything to pass. When they get yellow honey to eat they speak the truth. When they are deprived of god's sweet food they speak untruth. They flit about on wings and sprinkle their hair with white meal. Hermes can amuse himself with them.'[1] They were connected with the bees, which in folk-lore always had mysterious powers. The bees still fly about the sunny slopes of Parnassos and today build their hives in the ancient, sacred fountain of Kassotis, above the temple of Delphi.

Hermes, in a familiar story, stole Apollo's cattle and appeased his anger by giving him the seven-stringed lyre which he had made from the shell of a tortoise. Hermes, always the cunning, resourceful god, says in the *Hymn to Hermes*,

> I seek to be friendly with you both in thought and word,
> Now you know well all things in your heart since you sit
> Foremost among the deathless gods, O son of Zeus,
> And are goodly and strong . . .
> But since, as it seems, your heart is strangely set on playing
>   the lyre,
> Chant and play upon it, and give yourself merriment,
> Taking this as a gift from me.[2]

The Cretans were believed to have a special knowledge of religious rites and ceremonies and the hymn tells:

> Phoebus Apollo pondered in his heart
> What men he should bring in to be his ministers
> In sacrifice and to serve him in rocky Pytho.

[1] *Hesiod and Homeric Hymns.* Quotation from *Hymn to Hermes.*
[2] Ibid. *Hymn to Hermes.*

> And while he considered, he became aware of a swift ship
>   on the wine-dark sea,
> In which were many men and goodly Cretans from Knossos,
> The city of Minos, they who do sacrifice
> To the prince and announce his decrees, whatsoever Phoebus
>   Apollo,
> Bearer of the golden blade, speaks in answer
> From his laurel below the dells of Parnassos.
> These men were sailing in their black ship for gain and profit
>   to sandy Pylos,
> And to the men of Pylos. But Phoebus Apollo met them:
> In the open sea he sprang upon their swift ship, like a dolphin
>   in shape,
> And lay there, a great awesome monster, and none of them
>   gave heed to understand
> But they sought to cast the dolphin overboard.
>   But he kept shaking
> The black ship every way and making the timbers quiver.[1]

Apollo led his priests to the sanctuary in the form of this friendly creature, which ever afterwards was associated with Delphi and was named delphine or dolphin.

Apollo was worshipped as a god who changed the attitude of men towards murder. Ancient feuds which endlessly called for the blood of those who were guilty were now capable of appeasement. The Erinyes, who once screamed for the blood of Orestes, were now transformed into benevolent spirits. It was through purification and repentance that atonement could be made for murder. After killing the serpent or Python, Apollo himself sought purification. In some stories he went to Crete, but the most familiar legend tells that he went to the vale of Tempe. Tempe is a great gorge between the mountains of Olympos and Ossa, down which the River Peneus flows, 160 miles away from Delphi by the old route. It is a famous pass and still the main entrance from Macedonia into the plains of Thessaly. After the dusty plains of Central Greece it is a haven of quiet beauty where the air is fresh and cool. Many trees shade the green waters of the river as it winds its way between the mountain walls. To poets this lovely place has become synonymous with a haven of rest and tranquillity. It was sacred to Apollo, and the

[1] Ibid. *Hymn to Apollo.*

laurels still grow there, which were once taken ceremoniously to garland the winners of the Pythian Games.

A scene which was a popular subject for many vase paintings, showed Apollo's dispute with Herakles, who attempted to steal the tripod. The story is one which illustrates the attitude of the Delphic Oracle to blood guilt. Herakles, the enormously strong hero of Greek legend, had been ordered by the oracle, to expiate the crime of murdering his wife and children, which he had done in a fit of madness. He was commanded to undertake the twelve labours for which he is so famous. Once again he committed murder and the Pythia refused to admit him to the oracle. In his anger he carried off the sacred tripod, but was compelled by Zeus to restore it. He was condemned to a year's nameless slavery in punishment for his crime.

As with all the gods, stories were told of Apollo's love for mortal maidens. Some of these were purely symbolic, like his love for Kyrene, told by the people of the colony of Kyrene in North Africa, to account for their foundation. Kyrene was said to be the daughter of the hero-king Hyseus. She was not like other girls, who loved to work at the loom among the women of the household, but spent the days hunting and guarding her father's flocks. One day, as she was fighting a lion with her bare hands, Apollo saw her and immediately fell in love with her. 'He caught her up and in a golden car bore away the huntress maiden to the place where he made her queen of a land rich in flocks, yea richest of all the lands in the fruits of the field, that her home might be the third part of the mainland of earth'[1]—in other words, Africa, or Lybia, as it was then called.

Most of the love stories of Apollo were not such happy ones. There was Daphne, who was pursued by Apollo and turned into a laurel by Mother Earth; and Kassandra, the daughter of King Priam of Troy, to whom Apollo gave prophetic powers. When she repulsed him he was unable to take back his gift, but turned it to a curse which said that no one would ever believe her. There was another old fairy-story about the Cumaean Sibyl, who was loved by Apollo. He would have given her the gift of immortality but she repulsed him, so he said that she would live as long as the grains of dust in her hand, growing older and older. She shrivelled up so much that they hung her

[1] Pindar. *Pythian Ode*, IX.

up in a bottle. When children knocked on the bottle, and asked: 'Sibyl, what do you want?' the faint reply came, 'I want to die.'

The most famous story of all, however, was the account of the birth of Asklepios, who as the divine founder of medicine was another aspect of Apollo, himself a healer. Apollo loved Koronis 'the crow maiden', daughter of King Phlegyas, 'the fiery red'. While she was pregnant she gave herself, secretly, to a guest in her father's house, a mortal lover called Ischys. The raven, which was the favourite bird of Apollo, brought him the news. In those days the raven was a white bird, but in his anger Apollo turned it black, and sent his sister Artemis to kill the unfaithful girl. Many women of the Plegyans died with her and there was a great pestilence. As the funeral pyres blazed, Apollo said, 'I can no longer endure it that my son should perish with his mother.' He then snatched his unborn child from the flaming pyre, and took him to the wise centaur, Cheiron, who brought him up and taught him medicine and the use of herbs.

And thus all those that came unto him, whether they were plagued with infected sores or had limbs wounded by shining bronze or stones hurled by enemies, or suffered the hurts of summer heat or winter cold—all these he cured, freeing each from his pain, some with soothing ointments and some with gentle draughts or else he hung their limbs with powerful charms, or by the skill of surgery he restored them to health.[1]

In Epidaurus, where there was a hospital dedicated to Asklepios, and where the most famous ancient theatre is to be found in Greece today, they told another story, saying nothing about the unfaithfulness and death of Koronis, but simply that he was born there, in the sanctuary.

Eventually, Asklepios, forgetting his sacred mission of curing the ills of mankind, was 'beguiled by glittering gold'. In return for a great reward, he restored Hippolytus, son of Theseus, to life; and in so doing usurped the prerogative of the gods, who alone had power over life and death. Zeus in his anger killed him with a fiery thunderbolt. In return Apollo, powerless to avenge himself on his immortal father, requited his son's death

[1] Pindar. *Pythian Ode*, III.

by the killing of the Kyklopes who had made the thunderbolts used by Zeus. Once again Apollo had to make atonement and he stayed as a slave with Admetos, King of Pherai, minding his cattle for eight years, before he could return to Delphi undefiled. The sentence was an easy one as Admetos was a just and kindly man, and he was grateful to his serf for the way his cattle throve. Apollo wished to help his master and when he heard that the Moirai, the fates, gave Admetos only a short time to live, he softened their hearts with wine and they consented to let Admetos live on if someone would die in his stead. Alkestis, his wife, agreed to die in his place, and Euripides, in one of his few tragedies with a happy ending, tells the moving story of her death and rescue from the grave by Herakles.[1]

The stories and legends about Apollo, some of them fanciful and some of them dramatic and full of allegory, were sung by choirs at Delphi, or told to visitors in the stoas of the city; but there was a stranger story than any of those about the origin of Apollo and his oracle, which puzzled visitors in ancient days, and still causes controversy.

When Pausanias was at Delphi in the second century A.D. he was told that Boeo, a Phokian woman who composed a hymn for Delphi, said that the oracle was set up to the god by Olen and some others who came from the Hyperboreans, and that Olen was the first who delivered oracles in hexameters. Boeo had written the following lines, Pausanias said, 'Here Pegasus and divine Agaieus, sons of the Hyperboreans, raised to thy memory an oracle . . .' and enumerating other Hyperboreans, she mentions at the end of her hymn, Olen. 'And Olen who was Phoebus' first prophet. And first put in verse the ancient oracles.'[2]

The Hyperboreans were the people who lived in 'the land that lieth beyond the blast of the cold North wind', and in the hymns of praise sung to visitors at the festivals at Delphi, it was sometimes told that Apollo particularly loved these fair dwellers in the north, who sacrificed asses to the god.

For ever in the feasts and hymns Apollo has especial joy, and laughs as he looks on the strange beasts in their rampant lewdness. And the

[1] Euripides. *Alkestis.*
[2] Pausanias. *Description of Greece.*

muses are not strangers to their lives, but everywhere there is the shrill sound of the pipes and the movement to and fro of maidens dancing, and binding golden bay leaves in their hair they sing and feast merrily.[1]

Every year for the three dark winter months, Apollo left the sanctuary in Delphi, and went to the north to live with his Hyperborean worshippers. There was once an old poem of Alkaeus, written about 600 B.C. which said that when Apollo was born Zeus intended him to go straight to Delphi to dispense the law to the Hellenes, but instead he made use of his swan-chariot to fly to the Hyperboreans where he stayed for a year. Other accounts say that he went to them on the back of a winged griffon.

The land of the Hyperboreans was regarded by many ancient writers as a fairy-tale land, like the Isles of the Blessed, where there was neither old age, nor famine, nor pestilence; a land of everlasting youth and beauty where golden men and women danced and feasted perpetually.[2] There was other evidence for the existence of the Hyperboreans, however. At the time of Herodotus strange gifts were sent, carefully wrapped in straw, to the sanctuary of Apollo at Delos. They came from the Hyperboreans, in the land of the black and white poplars, and Plutarch said that in olden times these sacred gifts were brought down the road from Tempe, accompanied by flutes and pipes and the lyre. Once, it was said, the gifts were brought by Hyperborean maidens, but they were molested on the way, and ever since then it had become the custom to pass the gifts on from nation to nation on their way south.

Long before Herodotus wrote his histories in the fifth century B.C. men had walked down the old trade routes from the North Sea carrying their amber to the rich cities of the south, and they may have worshipped a god very like Apollo, and have sent their gifts to his temple each year. Robert Graves quotes Diodorus Siculus as saying that the Hyperboreans were British, and suggests that once Delos was the centre of a cult incorporating Palestine, Britain and Athens, and that visits were constantly exchanged.[3] Diodorus stated that there was a great

[1] Pindar. *Pythian Ode*, X.
[2] Cf. Diodorus Siculus. *World History*: II. 47.
[3] Robert Graves. *Greek Myths*, 1958.

temple to Apollo in Britain, which may have been at Avebury.

Whether there was any real evidence of Apollo's connection with Britain or not, it was a pleasant and conceited fancy of romantic poets that Apollo and his muses came to that country. Thomas Gray wrote:

> Woods that waved o'er Delphi's steep,
> Isles, that crown the Egaean deep,
> Fields, that cool Ilissus laves,
> Or where Maeander's amber waves,
> In lingering lab'rinths creep.
> How do your tuneful Echoes languish
> Mute, but to the voice of Anguish?
> Where each old poetic Mountain
> Inspiration breathes around;
> Every shade and hallow'd Fountain
> Murmer'd deep a solemn sound;
> Till the sad nine in Greece's evil hour
> Left their Parnassus for the Latian plains.
> Alike they scorn the pomp of tyrant Power,
> And coward Vice, that revels in her chains,
> When Latium had her lofty spirit lost,
> They sought, O Albion! next thy sea-encircled coast.[1]

The conflicting stories of the origins of the worship of Apollo have led to long disputes by scholars about whether he was originally an Asiatic god or a northern god, and the two centres of his worship, Delphi and Delos, each have their own characteristic stories. Professor Nilsson and others claim that his worship spread from Lycia in Asia Minor, where the name Apollo Lykios arose and where ancient Hittite inscriptions to Apulunas have been found. At the time of Homer there was little to connect him with Delphi, and his worship was centred on Crete and the Ionian Island of Delos. R. E. Willets believes that the strong links between Delphi and Crete point to the origins of his worship on that island in pre-Hellenic times.[2] He was worshipped there under many names, including that of Apollo Smintheus—the mouse-killer—a purely Cretan word that was not Greek.[3]

[1] Thomas Gray. *Progress of Poesy*, 1950.
[2] R. E. Willets. *Cretan Cults and Festivals*, 1962.
[3] Cf. Strabo. *Geographies*: 13. 1. 48.

Others, like Professor Cook, favour the northern origin of Apollo, pointing to Hyperborean traditions and see Apollo as a Dorian tribal deity, connected with the ancient gatherings known to the Dorians as *apellae*.[1]

Professor Guthrie quotes A. H. Krappe as saying: 'Many of the most bitter controversies concerning the nature and origin of Apollon could have been avoided, had it been realized that the Apollon of the classical epoch is as much of a compound as was the Hellenic nation itself.'[2]

All the arguments are pedantic ones when it is realized that to the Dorians coming down into Greece from the north or among Ionian Greeks in the south, the name of the god mattered little. It was the same god they worshipped, however his rites varied. The god was real, only man's concepts were different. To the Greeks, his origin was of small importance; the only thing that mattered was that he was the most splendid and awful of the Olympian gods. As men's concept of him changed, he came to be regarded as one of the noblest gods of the Greeks, and it was with real, religious veneration that he was welcomed back to Delphi each spring. In the third century B.C. Kallimachos described his coming: 'No longer is the god afar off. Make ready, Ye young men, for the song and the choir. Not to everyone doth Apollo manifest himself, but only to the good. Whoso shall have seen him, great is he; small the man who hath not seen him.'

In the words of Plutarch: '. . . The god Apollo is not several, made up of an infinite number of things, as we are. He is with reference to no time, but only to the eternal, the immovable and timeless. There is nothing before, nor after, nor more, nor past, nor older, nor younger; but He being One with the "Now" hath filled up the "Ever".'[3]

[1] A. B. Cook. *Zeus*, Vol. II.
[2] W. K. C. Guthrie. *The Greeks and Their Gods*.
[3] Plutarch. *Moralia*.

6 · *Dionysos*

AT the beginning of November, as the days get shorter and the first winter snows fall on the high peaks of Parnassos, Apollo leaves his temple at Delphi to fly away to the Hyperboreans. There he will spend the three months of winter perhaps in the perpetual summer of the Elysian fields or, as some have thought, bringing inspiration for winter concerts to choirs and musicians in the cold northern lands. The summer dies and the last tourists leave, just as those who came to consult the oracle left many years ago. The people of Delphi bring in the wood for winter fires and the shepherds on the high meadows start to gather their flocks for the long walk down the mountain paths to shelter in the towns and villages.

For three months the oracle was *nefaste* and could not speak, and the daily services of the priests of Apollo about the temple ceased, for a quiet period of waiting for the glorious return of Apollo at the beginning of February. Yet the worship at the sanctuary was not entirely suppressed during the winter, as it was then that the most mysterious of all the Greek gods came into his own. For nine months of the year Apollo was supreme but for three months it was Dionysos, the younger brother of Apollo, who reigned over Delphi.

By one of the most paradoxical aspects of Greek religious thought, Dionysos the mystical, ecstatic, unreasonable god shared the sanctuary at Delphi with Apollo, the supreme god of reason and light and harmony.

Dionysos was a newcomer to the Greek pantheon of Olympian gods. At the time of Homer, he was not one of the twelve aristocratic Olympian deities, but a foreign, barbarian god. He was then of little importance, but to ordinary people there were links through him with a dim past, when ancient rites were performed. At some time, during the early history of the Greeks, his worship spread throughout the land, always against considerable opposition. The sensible Greeks thought to tame

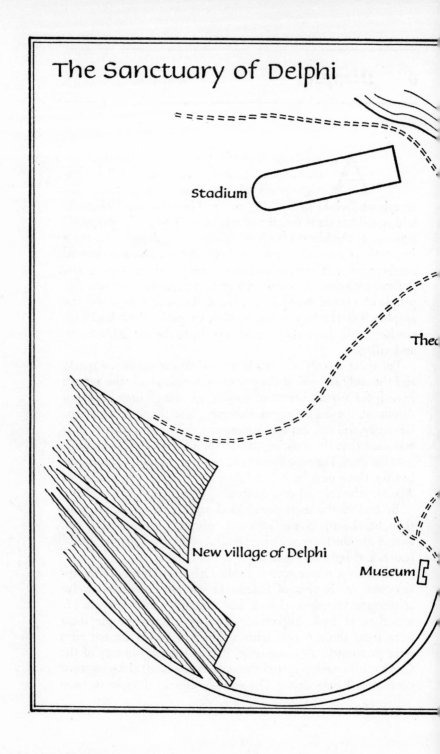

The Sanctuary of Delphi

Stadium

Thea

New village of Delphi

Museum

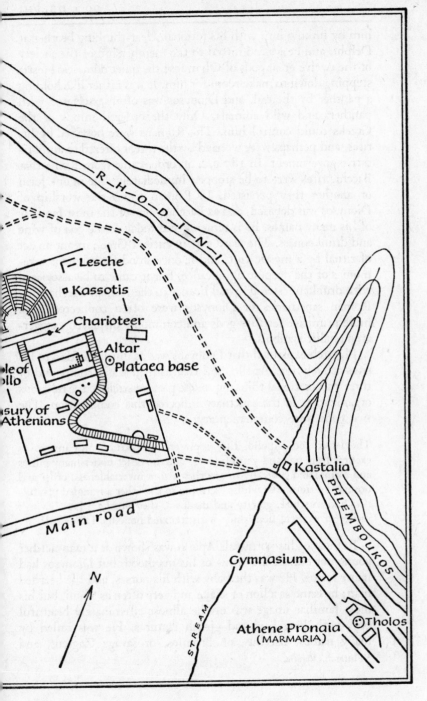

Lesche

Kassotis

Charioteer

Altar

Plataea base

le of
llo

sury of
Athenians

R—H—O—D—I—N—I

Kastalia

PHLEMBOUKOS

Main road

Gymnasium

N

STREAM

Tholos

Athene Pronaia
(MARMARIA)

F

him by linking him with his rational, clear-thinking brother at Delphi, and he was admitted to the membership of the society of the twelve great gods of Olympos; the quiet domestic Hestia stepping down to make room for him. It was rather like holding a panther by the tail, and Dionysos was often associated with panthers and wild animals. Only the ordered minds of the Greeks could control him. The Romans were horrified by his rites, and perhaps were worried by the threat offered to authoritative government. In 187 B.C. an order came from Rome that Bacchic rites were to be stopped immediately, but in one form or another they persisted. In Roman times the worship of Dionysos was debased, and as Bacchus, one of the most familiar of his many names, he is remembered today as the god of wine and drunkenness. The word *orgy* in ancient Greek meant an act of ritual by a mystic cult, and it once stood for religious ceremonies of the deepest significance, but it came to be associated with drunkenness and sexual licence in the Roman Bacchanalia. Roman sanctuaries of Dionysos were often connected with more primitive fertility gods and commonly displayed exaggerated phallic symbols.

Plutarch explained that Dionysos was as much entitled to his rites at Delphi as Apollo, and that as man was a compound of three parts rational thinking to one part mysticism, the religious organization in the sanctuary reflected this combination. The two gods were complementary.

The latter god, Apollo, they represent in pictures and images as exempt from age and youthfulness, but the other under many guises and forms: and generally to one they assign invariableness, order and unmixed seriousness; whilst ascribing to the other a mingled playfulness and mischief, gravity and madness, they proclaim him 'Evius', inciter of women, flourishing with frenzied honours, Dionysos![1]

In most of his portrayals Apollo was shown as a man neither young nor old, in the prime of his manhood, but Dionysos had many forms. He was the baby with his nurses, and the bearded man; he came as a lion or snake and very often as a bull, but his most familiar image was of the almost effeminately beautiful boy, with long hair and girlish features. He was called by many names, Bacchus, or Bromios, or savage Zagreus, and

[1] Plutarch. *Moralia*.

hundreds more, as he was the most diverse and complex of all the gods.

As part of our hidden nature, Dionysos, in one form or another, has appeared to men at all times in history, and as a mystic he cannot be explained in rational terms. Professor Guthrie says:

The worship of Dionysos is something which can never be wholly explained. . . . From the story of his miraculous birth onwards, there are strange, unique elements in his myths and cult for which it is impossible to find exact analogies. This in itself helps to account for the extraordinary hold that he obtained over mens' minds, a hold not relinquished even today, so that the task of describing him is made more difficult by the fact that many modern writers have inevitably had their emotions stirred either to sympathy or hostility by this incomprehensible and imperious stranger in their midst.[1]

He was the god of rebirth who brought a promise of immortality; he was the joyful bringer of fertility and giver of all gifts, but he was also a god of death, who reigned during winter months. He was a god of quietness, when all animals were tame and innocent, but also a raging, terrifying god of madness, an eater of flesh and tearer of living creatures.

The early historians and poets of Greece told of the origins of Dionysos in Thrace and Asia Minor, where Herodotus says he was worshipped under the name of Sabos. Wandering bands of his followers came into Greece from the north, through Macedonia and the vale of Tempe, bringing their orgiastic dances and wild, ecstatic worship, so foreign to the official religious ceremonies of the Greek people. In the greatest of all Euripides plays, the *Bacchae*, Dionysos said that he came from;

> The wide hot plains where Persian sunbeams play,
> The Bactrian war-holds, and the storm oppressed
> Clime of the Mede and Araby the Blest,
> And Asia all, that by the salt sea lies. . . .
> And now I come to Hellas, having taught
> All the world else my dances and my rites
> Of mysteries, to show me in men's sight
> Manifest God.[2]

[1] W. K. C. Guthrie. *The Greeks and Their Gods.*
[2] Euripides. *Bacchae.* Translated by Gilbert Murray, 1911.

Dionysos was originally an eastern god and according to legend he taught his rites in Asia before coming to Greece. He is often pictured accompanied by tigers and leopards and other exotic animals familiar to him. It was to Asia that he returned many years later, as Alexander the Great was believed by many of his followers to be a re-incarnation of Dionysos. The triumphal journey through Persia into India was interpreted as a re-conquest of his old territory by Dionysos.

In Euripides' play, when Dionysos came with his band of women followers, the Maenads, he was on his way to Delphi, but first he went to Thebes, for it was there that he intended to introduce his worship to the Greeks. In the legends told about the god, Thebes was his birth-place. His mother Semele was a mortal, the daughter of Kadmos, King of Thebes. In Thrace, or Phrygia, as it was called then, the name Semele was also the name of a god of the underworld. Zeus, the father of so many gods and heroes, fell in love with Semele, and she was about to bear his child. Once again the story tells of the jealousy of Hera, a theme that recurs many times in the tales of the gods. Hera disguised herself as the old nurse of Semele and urged her to ask Zeus to show himself in his real form, as a god. Semele was persuaded, and asked Zeus to grant her a favour. He agreed, swearing by the River Styx that he would grant her wish. This was an oath that neither gods nor men could break, and so when Semele asked that he should show herself in the same form as he appeared to Hera, he had to fulfil her request. The power and radiance of the gods was so great that no mortal could look on them and live, so when he appeared to Semele in his full glory she was destroyed immediately, in a flash of lightning. At the moment of her death, Zeus snatched Dionysos, his unborn son, from her and sewed him into his own thigh, or in some accounts he bound him there with golden bands. Eventually Dionysos was born from his father's thigh, and one of his many names afterwards was one meaning 'in-sewn'.

This simple story was of the kind usually told about the gods, but Dionysos was no ordinary god, and the myths and legends surrounding him were diverse and sometimes contradictory.

A story told by the Orphics, links Dionysos in his death and rebirth with Delphi. Orphism, derived from the legend of the famous singer Orpheus, was one of the most important mystery cults that existed in Greece. The legend of Orpheus and his wife, Eurydice, is very familiar, but the story of his death, told by the Roman poet, Ovid, is less widely known, and it links him with Dionysos.[1] Orpheus, who was a poet and prophet of Thrace, the original home of the Dionysian worship, was called the 'Chaplain of the Orgies' and his playing and singing were so sweet that the savage beasts, and even the trees, gathered round to hear him. The Maenads, followers of Dionysos, mocked him because he 'disdained women', and then killed him with the tools the field-workers had left behind, when they fled in fear from the raging women. Orpheus, when he died, went to the underworld to rejoin Eurydice, and lives for ever with her in the Elysian fields. Dionysos was so angry at the terrible death of Orpheus that he turned the Maenads into trees and left the country with a different band of followers.

Orphism developed out of the beliefs of the Pythagoreans, and it had a profound influence on men who thought deeply about religion; men who were not content to accept, without reservations, the official, state religious worship of the gods which followed the pattern laid down by Homer. The allegories of the Orphics were complex and hard to follow, but they connected Dionysos with life after death. They said that the giant Titans, who were strange beings borne by Mother Earth, had attacked the baby Dionysos as he played with his toys, and had torn him into seven pieces. They threw the pieces into a cauldron on a tripod, and boiled them. When the flesh was boiled they roasted it. Zeus then appeared and struck the Titans with his thunderbolts and gave the limbs of the baby god to Apollo. Apollo, obedient to the commands of Zeus, took the body in pieces to Delphi, and there placed them in his own sacred tripod. Some said that a part of it was hidden in a cradle or *liknon* and each year the child in the cradle is reborn.

The Orphic stories have many similarities with the legends of the Egyptian god, Osiris, who was torn into fourteen pieces, and the Greeks believed that he was the same god as Dionysos, under another name. When Plutarch served as high priest at Delphi, the Dionysian festivals were led by his friend Clea, and

[1] Ovid. *Metamorphoses*.

he once said to her: 'That indeed he is the same with Bacchos, who is more fitting to know than yourself, Clea, you who have headed the Bacchanals at Delphi, and have been initiated into the rites of Osiris ever since your childhood?'[1]

Clea was the chief priestess of the rites of Dionysos, a position which carried the title of Thyia, which means 'the ecstatically raging'. Thyia has the same meaning as the name Thyone which, as legend tells, was once given to Semele, the mother of Dionysos. In this story, Dionysos went in search of Semele in the underworld. He was guided to her with the aid of a strange path-finder, a phallus made of fig-wood. When he found her, he brought her back from the dead and made her immortal, giving her the new name of Thyone.

A quite different account of the arrival of Dionysos in Greece, is told in a seventh-century B.C. hymn. This time the worship originated from across the sea:

I will tell of Dionysos, the son of glorious Semele, how he appeared on a jutting headland by the shore of the fruitless sea, seeming like a stripling in the first flush of manhood: his rich dark hair was waving about him, and on his strong shoulders he wore a purple robe. Presently there came swiftly over the sparkling sea Tyrsenian pirates on a well-decked ship—a miserable doom led them on. When they saw him they made signs to one another and sprang out quickly and seizing him straightway put him on board their ship exultingly; for they thought him the son of heaven-nurtured kings. They sought to bind him with rude bonds, but the bonds would not hold him, and the withes fell away from his hands and feet: and he sat with a smile in his dark eyes. Then the helmsman understood all and cried out at once to his fellows and said:

'Madmen! What god is this whom you have taken and bind, strong that he is? Not even the well-built ship can carry him. Surely this is either Zeus or Apollo who has the silver bow, or Poseidon, for he looks not like mortal man but like the gods who dwell on Olympos. Come, then, let us set him free upon the dark shore at once: do not lay hands on him, lest he grow angry, and stir up dangerous squalls.'

So said he: but the master chid him with taunting words: 'Madman, mark the wind and help us hoist sail on the ship: catch all the sheets. As for this fellow we men will see to him: I reckon he is bound for Egypt or for Cyprus or to the Hyperboreans or further

[1] Plutarch. *Moralia.* On Isis and Osiris.

still. But in the end he will speak out and tell us his friends and all his wealth and his brothers, now that providence has thrown him in our way.'

When he had said this, he had mast and sail hoisted on the ship, and the wind filled the sail and the crew hauled taut the sheets on either side. But soon strange things were seen among them. First of all sweet, fragrant wine ran streaming throughout all the black ship and a heavenly smell arose, so that all the seamen were seized with amazement when they saw it. And all at once a vine spread out both ways along the top of the sail with many clusters hanging down from it, and a dark ivy-plant twined about the mast, blossoming with flowers, and rich berries growing on it; and all the thole-pins were covered with garlands. When the pirates saw all this, then at last they bade the helmsman to put the ship to land. But the god changed into a dreadful lion there on the ship, in the bows, and roared loudly: amidships also he showed his wonders and created a shaggy bear which stood up ravening, while on the forepeak was the lion glaring fiercely with scowling brows. And so the sailors fled into the stern and crowded bemused about the right-minded helmsman, until suddenly the lion sprang upon the master and seized him; and when the sailors saw it they leapt out overboard one and all into the bright sea, escaping from a miserable fate, and were changed into dolphins. But on the helmsman Dionysos had mercy and held him back and made him altogether happy, saying to him:

'Take courage good friend; you have found favour with my heart. I am Boisterous Dionysos whom Cadmus' daughter Semele bare of union with Zeus.'[1]

Dionysos was the god of wine, but not the god of drunkenness. The Greeks were well aware of the undignified behaviour of those who drank too much, or drank their wine unmixed, as vase-paintings show. They were abstemious people, who usually drank wine mixed with water, but they believed that the use of wine, like the eating of bread, was an act of civilized men that raised them above savagery. They were also aware of how the wine brought freedom from restraint and could help produce surrender to the influence of a god, which the worship of Dionysos involved.

As they were first introduced into Greece the rites of Dionysos were alien to the sensible, clear-thinking people that the

[1] *Hesiod and Homeric Hymns.*

Greeks considered themselves to be. 'Here it comes, creeping on us like a fire, This Bacchic outrage, a disgrace in the eyes of Greece,' Pentheus says in *Bacchae*.

It was not only women who followed Dionysos, but the rites of a mystic god were more difficult for men who distrusted emotional and ecstatic abandon. Even in an enlightened age, women have been tied to dull domestic chores; to them the rule of the home and children and the domestic hearth have been more important than the affairs of men. The world of politics, commerce and war were less significant than the world of people and the life of the family. Dionysos offered them freedom and an escape to a wider communion with god and nature. Dressed in fawn-skins and bearing the tall wands, with a pine cone at the top, called *thyrsa*, they left their looms and their kitchens to follow the beautiful young man, who was child and lover in one, and abandoned themselves to the movements of the dance. Following the torches as they dipped and swayed in the darkness, they climbed mountain paths with heads thrown back and eyes glazed, dancing to the beat of the drum which stirred their blood. Delphi was once the scene of these rituals.

> Aye over Delphi's rock-built diadem
> Thou yet shall see him leaping with his train
> Of fire across the twin-peaked mountain-plain,
> Flaming darkness with his mystic wand,
> And great in Hellas.

In the state of *ekstasis* or *enthousiasmos*, they abandoned themselves, dancing wildly to the roll of the drums and calling '*Euoi!*' At that moment of intense rapture they became identified with the god himself, and tore to pieces any creatures which crossed their path. They saw them as an incarnation of the god and in eating the flesh, they became filled with his spirit and acquired divine powers. After all this, came the silence, the rapture when all nature seemed blessed; the water in the springs was wine; milk and honey flowed from the ground and all the wild creatures came to be caressed and loved. The chorus in Euripides' play sings about this, in what is probably the only contemporary account of an actual religious ritual:

The treasury of the Athenians. Rebuilding was possible because nothing was interchangeable and every stone had its carefully planned place and fitted nowhere else.

The treasury of the Athenians, front view. The only treasury standing now, where once there were many.

The Portico of the Athenians, erected in front of the polygonal wall to commemorate their sea victories. The pillars were re-erected in 1880 after being hidden for more than a thousand years.

Its proud inscription: *The Athenians have dedicated this portico with the arms and figureheads taken from their enemies at sea.*

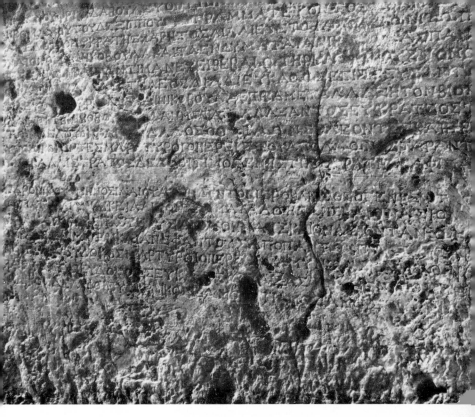

One of the hundreds of inscriptions carved on the polygonal wall, many of them telling of the manumission of slaves.

One of the few surviving examples of a hymn accompanied by ancient musical notation, on the wall of the treasury of the Athenians.

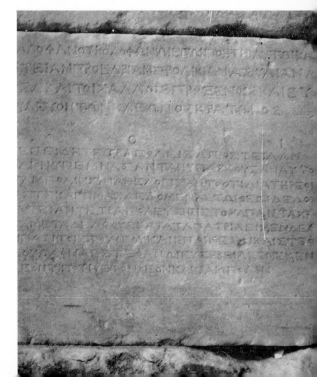

The great polygonal retaining wall of
the temple platform, built to withstand
earthquakes and rock falls for
thousands of years.

The foundations of the temple of Apollo. ▷
Massive blocks were placed one above the
other to withstand the ravages of nature,
but were displaced by men who sought the
precious iron bars which tied them in place.

△ The block shown to
tourists every day as the
site of the original
oracular tripod.

▷

The search for the true
omphalos goes on, and
there are several
contenders for the
honour amongst the
stones which lie in the
grass. This stone near
the treasury of the
Athenians might be the
original one.

Here near the southern foundations within the temple, quite at one side, stood a little structure, the *adyton,* sanctuary of the oracle, and very old in origin.

Marble seats for spectators, part of
the restoration of the stadium by
Herodes Atticus during Roman
times. The Delphic stadium is one of
the best preserved in Greece.

O glad, glad on the mountains
To swoon in the race out worn,
When the holy fawn-like clings
And all else sweeps away,
To the joy of the red quick fountains,
The blood of the hill-goat torn,
The glory of wild-beast ravenings
Where the hill tops catch the day;
To the Phrygian, Lydian, mountains!
Tis Bromius leads the way.

Then streams the earth with milk, yea, streams
With wine and nectar of the bee
And through the air dim perfume steams
Of Syrian frankincense; and He
Our leader, from his thyrsus spray
A torch light tosses high and higher,
A torch light like a beacon fire,
To waken all that faint and stray
And sets them leaping as he sings
His tresses rippling to the sky,
And deep beneath the Maenad cry
His proud voice rings: 'Come, O ye Bacchae come!'

Will they ever come to me, ever again,
The long long dances,
On through the dark till the dim stars wane?
Shall I feel the dew on my throat, and the stream
Of wind in my hair? Shall our white feet gleam
In the dim expanses?
Oh, feet of a fawn to the greenwood fled,
Alone in the grass and the loveliness;
Leap of the hunted, no more in dread.
Beyond the snares and the deadly press.[1]

These rites are inconceivable to us and impossible to explain rationally, but as the whole worship was irrational in the purest sense it is not really possible to explain it in everyday words. A more controlled description of the ecstasy of this kind was given by a writer called Aristides, who wrote:

It was a sort of sense of contact and a clear realization that the god himself had come; an intermediate state between sleeping and waking, a desire to look and at the same time a fear that he would go away

[1] Euripides. *Bacchae*.

first; a listening and hearing half in dream, half awake; the hair on end and tears of joy and an inward swelling with delight—what human beings could find words to describe it? Those who are of the initiated will understand and recognize it.[1]

The ecstasy which the followers of Dionysos experienced was a rage or madness known as mania. The name Maenad, which was given to Dionysian women, is derived from the same root as the word 'maniac', but with an older meaning. Socrates described this kind of madness as sacred. In it the soul left the body to achieve union with a god. We sometimes remark on the kinship between genius and insanity, and in ancient Greece, madness was not clearly separated from inspiration. Plato said: 'There is a madness which is a divine gift; the greatest of blessings have come to us in madness. For prophecy is madness and the prophetess at Delphi . . . has conferred great benefits on Hellas, yet in her senses few or none.'[2]

There are many stories of the birth and persecution and, sometimes, the killing of Dionysos, and of his rebirth. They were stories which were full of hidden allegory to his initiates, but his persecution and triumph had a historical origin as well. The mystic worship from Asia, with its disturbing effect on women in particular, was never well received by ordinary, matter-of-fact men, and it is not surprising that there was opposition to the orgiastic, uncontrolled rites of Dionysos. Euripides' play probably reflected truthfully the reaction of rulers to the insidious influence in their midst. It is a reaction which is personal as well as political, as men have always tended to fear and reject the mystic part of their own nature.

In the play, when Dionysos came to Thebes, Kadmus had given his kingdom to his son Pentheus, as he himself had become too old to rule. The sisters of Semele did not believe that Dionysos was the son of Zeus. They said that Semele mated with a mortal man and, when found pregnant, Kadmus, her old father, blamed the shame on Zeus to protect her name. And, they proclaimed, Semele's lie drew down on her the divine wrath, and that is why Zeus' thunderbolt struck her dead. Dionysos then drove the sisters mad because of their doubts

---

[1] Quoted by G. Misch in *A History of Autobiography in Antiquity*, 1951.
[2] Plato. *Apology*.

about his divinity. The first reaction of the family of Semele was a normal, reasonable one, and one which anyone today might have, when faced by wild stories of supernatural activities.

Pentheus, the King of Thebes, represents the sensible, ordinary man, scornful of mysteries, and suspicious of the effeminate, girl-faced, pretty young man who had so stirred up the women of his household that they had become mad. He also suspected that it was all an excuse for sexual licence and lust. Pentheus arrests Dionysos and has him brought before him for questioning. Dionysos is treated with contempt, his long hair is cut and his staff taken away from him, but during the questioning scene his power increases until Pentheus is completely under his spell. There follows an atmosphere of mounting horror, until Pentheus is deluded into watching the Bacchic rites, and is finally torn to pieces by his own family; his mother bearing his bloody head back to the palace, thinking it is the head of a lion. The chorus sings sadly of the terror that came to Pentheus because he denied the god:

> Is it so hard a thing to see,
> That the spirit of God, whate'er it be,
> The law that abides and changes not, ages long,
> The Eternal and Nature born—these things be strong.
> What else is wisdom? What man's endeavour
> Or God's high grace so lovely and so great?
> To stand from fear set free, to breathe and wait.
> To hold a hand uplifted over Hate;
> And shall not loveliness be loved for ever?[1]

Dionysos, in his myths, was twice born, and Delphi is associated with both his death and rebirth. In the *adyton* lay his tomb, connected with the most sacred function of the oracle. There was once a stone beside the golden statue of Apollo, which resembled a simple step, and it was said that it had an inscription: 'Here lies in death, Dionysos the son of Semele.'

Some modern archaeologists have suggested that the *omphalos* itself was a representative of a grave, and it certainly resembles the ancient *tholos* tombs of the Mycenaean people. There are

[1] Euripides. *Bacchae.*

links, too, between Dionysos and far earlier beliefs; one story said that he was the son of Deukalion. Deukalion was the Greek Noah, who at the time of the flooding of the world, landed in his ark above Delphi, on Parnassos. Dionysos perished in the flood and the fruits of the earth died with him. After the flood had subsided, he was revived in the shape of a vine, newly fertilized by the rains, bringing the blessing of wine to mankind. This story has links with the biblical story of Noah, who planted a vineyard when he came out of the ark and 'drank of the wine'.

The primitive, orgiastic worship of Dionysos was eventually refined and made decorous by sober Greeks in the practice of state religious observances. In Athens there was, each year, a symbolic ceremony of marriage between the wife of the 'King' Archon and Dionysos, and in the villages there were rural Dionysia with communal drinking, merrymaking and bawdy humour, but there was little of the old sacred possession of enthusiasm. It was, perhaps, only in Delphi where the ancient rites were carried out in their original ecstatic form. Here it was a ceremony closely connected with the belief in immortality, about which religious philosophers speculated, but which was not part of the official Homeric religious doctrine.

In Athens the spirit of Dionysos turned into another, exciting, direction. The mummers, who told the story of the god, in company with the village girls, who were his Maenads and ecstatic dancers, were called 'goat-singers' or *tragodoi* and from them grew the theatre, and the first performances of tragedy. Under the influence of the god and certainly, at first, with the co-operation of the priests of Dionysos, the theatre as we know it developed. Originally its purpose was entirely religious, and the great plays of Greece were at first enacted to portray man's relationship with the divine structure of the universe. Even today, when an audience is drawn into the world created by a company of actors, and when, after a performance of great intensity, they leave the theatre exalted, and only slowly return to the real world outside, they have perhaps experienced that kind of possession, or enthusiasm, which is Dionysian.

In Greece today, the links with ancient theatre and religion are still very real. The Byzantine Greek Orthodox Church has many parallels with the ancient theatre of Dionysos. The screen which conceals the sanctuary has the same form, with three doors, as the *skena* of the ancient theatre. The priest is the actor and responds to the choir, or chorus, of two groups of seven, exactly as the religious dramas of the past were first presented.

It is not only in forms of ritual or in the theatre, or in the fact that Saint Dionysius, in the Christian calendar of saints, is reputed to have brought the art of wine-making to Greece, that the worship of Dionysos is still evident today. It is even sometimes found in ecstatic frenzy as well. All through history God-possession continues to appear, often accompanied by persecution. In medieval times there were many Christian heretics who revealed traces of Dionysian influence; among them were the Euchites or 'Enthusiasts' who formed a strong community in eleventh-century Thrace, the original home of Dionysos; and the Paulicians who became Mohamedan and were connected with the Whirling Dervishes; and even the Bogomil heretics who believed 'the Devil was entrenched in the soul and through ecstatic states the believer might raise himself to visions of God'. All of them were persecuted, but still the rites persisted. The Bulgars rebelled against their overlords, the Byzantine rulers, in 1186, and were called Bacchantic Christians. A contemporary account said that:

In a state of ecstasy they had divined that they should be free, and in this ecstasy they claimed that God had condoned the freedom of the Bulgarians. . . .

For a while the demented folk withdrew into themselves and suddenly, concentrating their minds more strongly, and in the fashion of epileptics they cried out, as if possessed by a god, in loud voices.[1]

In 1961, 775 years after the Byzantine trouble with Bacchantic Christians, in the parts of Macedonia where Greeks from Thrace have settled, an eye-witness wrote an account of the annual festival of Saint Constantine: 'The silence was broken by the heavy sound of the drum. . . . Every so often the cry of some god-possessed initiate would break forth. An initiate uttering ecstatic cries . . . would begin to dance or rather to beat his feet monotonously and vigorously, intensifying the

[1] Katerina Kakouri. *Dionysiaka*, 1963.

ecstasy that had taken possession of his being.' Another account of these same people tells that 'when the dance was at its height, many folk broke away in their joy and ran up the mountainside'.[1]

The actions of modern ecstatic worshippers seem far removed from the worship in the sanctuary of Delphi. Here, certainly, the rites of Dionysos were once celebrated in all their savage mystery, but there were some wiser men, who could find a spiritual truth when they sought it, far above the superstitious, primitive festivals some of which still stay with us.

The uniting of Dionysos with Apollo is a paradox not only because of the difference between the two gods, but because, to conservative Greeks, the greatest sin against the gods was *hubris*, the sin of man usurping their privileges. At the time of belief in the original Olympian deities, and Apollo was among them, it was forbidden for man in his pride to aspire to reach their divine stature, but the followers of Dionysos became one with their god, and through him could achieve immortality. When his little daughter died, gentle Plutarch wrote to his wife:

About that which you have heard, dear heart, that the soul once departed from the body vanishes and feels nothing. I know that you give no belief to such assertions because of those sacred and faithful promises given in the mysteries of Dionysos, which we who are of that brotherhood know. We hold it firmly for an undoubted truth that our soul is incorruptible and immortal. We are to think [of the dead] that they pass to a better place and a happier condition. Let us behave ourselves accordingly, outwardly by an ordered life, while within all should be pure, wise, incorruptible. . . . Is God so petty, so attached to the trifling that he will take the trouble to create souls if we have nothing divine in us, nothing that resembles him, nothing lasting or sure, but all of us fades like a leaf?[2]

As far as we know, Plutarch knew nothing about Christianity, but the mysticism of the more enlightened followers of Dionysos prepared them to accept that new and exalted religion, which the orthodox pagans, believing in the strict hierarchy of Olympian gods, would have found difficult.

[1] Katerina Kakouri, *Dionysiaka*.
[2] Quoted by Edith Hamilton in *The Echo of Greece*.

To the Jews, who persecuted the Christians, Christianity was a heresy, because it was akin to the mysticism of the Greeks. Abraham Heschel in 1962 said: 'The root of ecstatic experiences in ancient religion lies in a thirst to become possessed with a god, or to become one with a god. . . . Such a thirst to become one with God, the supreme aspiration of many mystics, is alien to the biblical man. To him the term "Union with God" would be a blasphemy.'[1]

There was a saying among some followers of the Orphic mysteries that Dionysos was destined to overthrow Zeus and become the last great ruler of the gods. Perhaps the allegory implied that they saw dimly the coming of a newer and more gentle religion which was to include a great deal of that mysticism.

[1] Abraham Heschel. *The Prophets*, 1962.

EVERY day minor priests of the temple attended to their duties, keeping the courts clean, sweeping the steps of the sacred way and frightening the birds which fouled the statues. During Apollo's residence, the sacred fire was kept burning and the air was perfumed with incense. From time to time, following old customs, little rites and ceremonies were held, commemorating dimly remembered incidents of ancient history. One of these was the Aigle, which celebrated the great flood. It was told that when Zeus destroyed mankind in a great flood, Deukalion made a wooden box in which he stored all that was necessary. Zeus caused a great rain to fall, and Deukalion and his wife escaped in the box. After floating for nine days and nights they finally landed on Mount Parnassos. The shepherds of Parnassos followed the wolves up the mountain when the flood came, and there they built a town called Lykorea, or Wolf-Town. It was from here that the Delphians came, to found their city, perhaps at the same time as the worship of Apollo was introduced. There were certain hereditary priests of the temple called the *Hosioi*, who said that they were descendants of Deukalion and they took part in the public performance of sacrifices. Plutarch says that they also offered a secret sacrifice to Dionysos at certain times.

Every year on Apollo's birthday, the seventh of February, or Bysios, there was a celebration to welcome him back from the Hyperboreans, called the Theoxenis, and a feast was held. On this day Apollo welcomed all the other gods to join in the rejoicing 'in these holy hours of Spring'. The festivities included a poetic competition and what appears to have been a vegetable show, as an inscription tells of the prize given to someone who exhibited the finest leek.

After Apollo had left in the autumn there was a secret ceremony, the awakening of the *Liknites*. This was carried out by the girls of Delphi under the leadership of the Thyia, the priestess of Dionysos. Plutarch says that the *Liknites* was 'repeatedly awakened' in the autumn. The significance of the ceremony was the rebirth of Dionysos, and the raising of him from the tomb where he had lain all the summer. Although we see the rebirth of life and nature in the spring after the winter, there is also another renewal of life in hot Mediterranean countries, when the long, hot drought of summer is followed by the first rains of the autumn. The grass starts to grow again and the country people plant their seeds for autumn crops. The rejoicing of the harvest festival is here closely connected with fertility and re-growth. Although we know of the festival, the rites themselves are obscure. The *Liknites* is 'he who is in the *liknon*', and the *liknon* was a winnowing fan, but it was also the name of a basket or cradle. It may have been the cradle of the baby Dionysos, but it was also connected with the *liknon* carried in festal processions on the head of a priestess. The basket contained mysterious objects which were connected with the fertility of the soil and of nature.

These were all private festivals, related to the observation of ritual ceremonies, but there were also the great public festivals which were important to the whole of Greece. Ever since Apollo was first worshipped at Delphi, there was a festival celebrated every eight years or, as it was called in those days, a nine-year festival. It was held in three parts, the first of which was the Stepterion. Plutarch described it as being, in part, a holy drama which enacted the combat of Apollo with the Python, and his subsequent flight to the vale of Tempe to be purified. It then showed his triumphant return to Delphi carrying the sacred laurel.

The paved road, known as the Sacred Way, winds up to the court in front of the temple doors where the high altar stands. Before it turns the corner of the polygonal wall, the bastion which supports the terrace of the temple, the path widens into an open space bordered with bases of statues and platforms for spectators. This circular esplanade was known as the 'threshing floor'. The threshing floor is one of the common sights of every village in Greece, where the sparse crops of grain are threshed by methods as old as Delphi itself. These flat spaces among the fields and on the hillsides were a convenient meeting-place for dancing and harvest festivals, and on them were once held the most primitive festivals of all; the rites and invocations to

G

Mother Earth to ensure bountiful crops. As a result, the name 'threshing floor' came to have special sanctity. On this 'place of the threshing floor', at the time of the Stepterion they built a hut or stage-set, representing a royal palace. A virgin boy was chosen to act the part of Apollo. He was selected from one of the noble families of Delphi and both his parents had to be living. With a group of his friends, accompanied by a sacred escort of women carrying torches, they went by night, in silence, up the Sacred Way to the hut of the threshing floor. One account said that the boy fired arrows into the hut where the Python was lurking. Other accounts do not mention the Python, but in all cases the torches were flung on to the hut, setting fire to it, and the whole party turned and ran away, without looking back. The boy acting the part of Apollo pretended to go into exile and, with his friends, made the long journey to Tempe on foot. This must have taken about a week. At Tempe they collected laurel branches and returned in procession, passing through various Greek states, who treated them with great respect and honour.

The laurel, sacred to Apollo, was carried with much ceremonial as, later in the year, it was used to make the crowns for the winners of the Pythian Games. Plutarch said: 'The youth who brings back the laurel of Tempe to Delphi is accompanied by a flute player; and they say that in olden times the sacred gifts of the Hyperboreans were sent to Delos with flute and pipes and the lyre.' Later writers have seen this remark as indicating in Plutarch's mind, a link between Apollo and his northern origin.

Plutarch, who was very much opposed to superstitious practices, did not like the belittling of Apollo suggested by this festival and quoted his friend, Cleombrotus, as saying: 'It is utterly ridiculous to suppose, my good friend, that Apollo after slaying the reptile, fled away to the other end of Greece, seeking after purification, and caused a few pitchers to be poured over him.' He believed that the hut built on the threshing floor was not a 'memorial of the lurking hole of the serpent, but of the habitation of some tyrant or king'.[1]

The second sacred festival of the eight-year period was the Herois, which was held in secret. Only the priestess of Diony-

[1] Plutarch. *Moralia.*

sos, the Thyia, and her assistants knew the rites, but they were connected in some way with the bringing-back to earth of Semele, the mother of Dionysos.

The Thyia was also connected with the third festival which was called Charila. Charila was the name of a heroine of the legendary past, and the story they told about her was that there was once a great drought, and as the crops were burnt up by the sun there was a terrible famine. The king, responsible for the welfare of his people, controlled the granary where the stores of barley and other grains were kept for just such an occasion as this. When the distribution started, the king found that there was not enough for everyone, so he gave the grain to the noblest families. An orphan girl, Charila, came and begged him to give her a little food, but the king was angry and threw his shoe at her. The poor girl went away and hanged herself. Immediately afterwards a plague came, in addition to the famine, and, on being consulted, the oracle announced that a ceremony must be instituted to propitiate the spirit of the dead girl. Every time the festival year came to Delphi, this was carried out. The 'king', who in democratic, republican Delphi, was played by a priest, sat before the temple and distributed barley and pulses to anyone who came by, whether citizen or stranger. The Thyia brought a doll to the 'king', who struck it with his shoe, and the priestess took the doll to the ravine, put a rope round its neck, and buried it at the supposed site of Charila's grave.

These festivals were accompanied by sacrifices to the god and a banquet was also held. There were, too, processions when the hymns of praise, known as Paeans, were sung to Apollo. Some choirs were extremely famous, and there were always crowds who gathered to hear them. Plutarch described an occasion when the choirs gathered to sing hymns to Apollo; the place was Delos, but there must have been very similar processions at Delphi. It gives a vivid impression of the difficulties of the director of a pageant of this kind.

The dancers and singers . . . were wont before to arrive disorderly; and the cause was, for the number of people that ran to see them, who made them sing straight away without any order . . . they left their apparel, and put on such vestments as they should wear in the procession and threw garlands of flowers on their heads, all at one present time.

Nicias, the Athenian, who was presenting the choirs from that city was ashamed of the disorder, and brought a bridge from Athens, so that the singers could assemble on a neighbouring island.

The bridge was set out with pictures and tables with gilding, with nosegays and garlands of triumph and excellently wrought tapestry . . . and at break of day the singers passed over it, singing all the way as they went in procession so nobly set forth, even unto the very temple of Apollo.[1]

In Delphi the choirs and processional trains formed themselves up in order, on the famous threshing floor, for a triumphant walk up to the temple. The *exedras*, or platforms, where the audience crowded, can still be seen round this open space.

From the earliest recorded history of Delphi, the great religious festivals were accompanied by music. There was a special competition for a Delphic *nome* or musical drama invented by a singer called Sakadas, which illustrated the fight between Apollo and the dragon. The rules of competition were strict. The performance was given by a flute player accompanied by the *kithara*, the ancestor of the guitar and the zither, and a salpinx, or trumpet, and was in five parts.

The first part had to represent Apollo inspecting the field of battle, followed by the challenge, when he shouted abuse. The third part was the actual combat scene, which was a wonderful opportunity for the composer to create dramatic effects. There were the sounds of gnashing of teeth and roaring, and above them all the whistle of the arrows.

This was followed by the *spondium*, the argument, which was a hymn to celebrate the god's victory, accompanied by the syrinx, or double pipe, representing the hissing of the dying snake. Finally, there was a gay celebration dance.

This sophisticated drama was invented in 586 B.C., but before then there were always competitions for hymn singing accompanied by the lyre or harp. The recorders of Delphi claimed that the first competition was won by Chrysthemis, a Cretan, possibly one of the priests Apollo first brought to the sanctuary. According to Pausanias every one of the worlds most famous poets at one time or another aspired to the honour of

[1] Plutarch. *Parallel Lives*, Nicias. Translated by Sir Thomas North, 1579.

competing at Delphi. 'Hesiod was not permitted to be a competitor because he had not learned to accompany his voice with a harp. Homer too went to Delphi to inquire what was necessary for him, and even had he learnt to play on the harp, the knowledge would have been useless to him, because of his being blind.'

Apart from repeating the traditional story that Homer was a blind singer, Pausanias' comment is interesting in view of some modern theories that the conductor of a choir in ancient days played an important part by using hand signals to indicate the pitch as well as the beat of a musical score. To be blind would have been a serious handicap to a singer under the circumstances, and may have disqualified competitors at Delphi.

In 590 B.C. after the First Sacred War there was a reorganization of the Pythian Festivals. Delphi was formally adopted as the centre of pan-Hellenic worship, and all the ceremonies and functions of the temple were examined and rules governing them were drawn up. It was agreed that in future there would be athletic events, modelled on Olympia, in addition to musical contests, and that these should be known as the Pythian Games. The Stepterion was held every eight years as before, but the other contests, which were no longer limited to events describing the life of Apollo, were now held more frequently. There was great building activity at this time, and above the temple the first stadium was erected.

Under the new administration, at the first Pythian games, prizes of money were given to the competitors, but this was not repeated, and afterwards the prize consisted only of a laurel wreath. In their home-country, on the other hand, the winners were adulated and given a hero's reception, and were often maintained at the expense of the state for the rest of their lives. Just as with the Olympic Games, the competitors represented the states which nurtured them and by winning they brought glory to their native country.

The first athletic events were the long course and double course for boys: a course being one length of the stadium, or 220 yards. Every year afterwards, new events were added, or old ones changed. In the musical events the flute was at one time regarded as the most important instrument. This flute as it is usually called in translations, was a reeded instrument called an *aulos*, and Pindar described it as being made of 'thin beat bronze'.[1] Although it had been used at the festivals for many years, after the first of the reorganized Pythian Games its use was stopped by the festival committee. 'They stopped singing to the pipes, as not pleasing to the ear. For singing to the pipes was a most gloomy kind of music,'[2] Pausanias said. At the time of Plutarch it was restored to favour, when its playing was not so lugubrious and in better keeping with the cheerful Greek temperament, and he says: 'For it was only recently that the flute gave forth its sound of merriment, in old times it drawled out in lamentations at funerals, and held this office (not a very respectable or cheerful one) at scenes of this kind.'[3]

A few years later horse races were started, in a special stadium or hippodrome built below Krissos, on the plain. These were among the most popular events, and attracted large numbers of competitors. We know from a poem of 466 B.C. that the charioteers had to cover a course twelve times and that the crowded stadium was extremely dangerous, especially at the turns. In the race held that year, forty charioteers fell or were thrown from their chariots.

Nearly a hundred years after the start of the new series of Pythian Games, a race, in full armour, was instituted. At this time, in 498 B.C., the Greek army tactics depended on the hoplites, soldiers who wore the traditional Greek plumed helmets and breastplates, and carried heavy shields and spears, in addition to their swords. The battle of Marathon was won by a charge of heavily armed hoplites. As there was no regular army, it was considered part of the accomplishment of all men that they should be skilled in battle. It was the same spirit which encouraged the sport of archery in English history.

In spite of the tremendous popularity of the athletic events, Delphi remained the home of the great musical festival and was the only place in Greece which awarded prizes, not only to poets and musicians, but to artists. It was the prototype of the art exhibition of modern Europe. 'For in this festival alone, we hear of the artists competing,' Professor Farnell says in *Cults of the Greek States*: 'The great Delphic celebration then was pre-

[1] Pindar. *Pythian Ode*, XII.
[2] Pausanias. *Description of Greece*, Phokis.
[3] Plutarch. *Moralia*.

eminently the consecration of the highest life of Hellas to Apollo.' The individual who competed at Delphi dedicated himself, either physically in the training for bodily perfection and beauty, or as a poet or musician. The whole person involved both aspects, and to Greek thinking there never was any conflict between the two.

The festivals of Apollo took place during the summer months, but when autumn came and Apollo left his sanctuary there was a change in the character of the celebrations held in Delphi. The hymns and songs that were sung to Apollo were paeans. Plutarch describes them as 'an orderly and discreet form of composition'. They represented 'satiety' in the sense of completeness, or a fulfilment of every need. Now a new kind of singing was heard. This was the dithyramb, with its irregular beat, which was sung in honour of Dionysos. Plutarch says: 'At the beginning of winter they revive the dithyramb and put a stop to the paean, invoking the second god for the space of three months in place of the first.'

As Dionysos was the god of the theatre, it is natural that the dithyramb should be connected so much with the chorus in ancient theatre. It is also believed to have had an effect on modern Greek music. Madame Nicoloudi, the choreographer of Aristophanes' the *Birds*, says that: 'The very characteristic Greek rhythms, which are basically lop-sided, have a lack of symmetry which perhaps gives Greek music its lively and primitive character.'[1]

The dithyramb was music which excited the listeners and made them want to dance, and dancing was essential to the worship of Dionysos and to his festivals at Delphi. The most important of these was the orgy held every two years, which was performed jointly by the girls of Athens and Delphi, who were known as Thyiads.

During the festival year, a team of fourteen girls and women from the best families in Athens was selected by the chief priest, to act as the Thyiads. Late in October they set out to walk the long, mountainous road to Delphi. The girls were not a select band of priestesses, different from the other women of Athens, but the daughters of citizens. It was not considered surprising that they should undertake an adventurous journey of nearly a

[1] Programme note on the music of the *Birds*.

hundred miles on foot, and Professor Seltman, who did so much to vindicate the status of women in classical Greece, said:

The young women and girls of Athens were assuredly tough. The once popular notion that Athenian females were dull, unenterprising creatures, as physically inadequate as though they had never stepped outside a convent or seraglio and therefore held in disdain by the men, is now ceasing to be maintained with conviction. The Thyiads are one more example—if such is really needed—of some temporary independence and audacious activity on the women's part.[1]

Pausanias wrote: 'Thyiads are Athenian women who annually go to Parnassos in concert with the Delphian women and cele-brate the orgies of Dionysos. These Thyiads hold dances on the road from Athens and elsewhere.' The people of the towns and villages on the road to Delphi, welcomed them as they passed through, and the dances of the Athenian girls must have been an event to which they looked forward eagerly. One of the towns was Panopeus, and there was a saying that 'Panopeus delighted in the dance' which Pausanias thought referred to the visit there of the Thyiads.

At last the girls arrived at Delphi some time during Novem-ber, and were met by their sister Thyiads from among the Delphians. It was only in Athens and Delphi that the women who took part in the ecstatic orgies of Dionysos were known as Thyiads, which indicated a strong link between the two com-munities.

The temple of Apollo was silent, and the Pythia no longer sat in the *adyton* bringing her messages to waiting consultants, but the tomb of Dionysos was also in the *adyton*, and here solemn rites would be held to restore him to life again.

One can imagine the scene in Delphi, a few evenings later. From the temple of Apollo the Thyiads went to the theatre, for this was the true temple of Dionysos. Sacrifices were made and there were preparations for the great celebration, when every participant shared in a mystical union with the god. Everyone who followed and joined in the enthusiasm and knew the ecstasy became at the same moment the god he worshipped.

The excitement in the theatre, as night fell and the setting sun brought a glow of flaming colour to the rocks high above,

[1] Charles Seltman. *The Twelve Olympians.*

was intensified by the beating of a drum. Wine was drunk in honour of the god, but only a little, for this was not drunkenness, but an increase in all the powers of perception and the beginning of relaxation from the ties of ordinary life. As darkness came, the young shepherds from Parnassos lighted torches and started up the path from the back of the theatre that went behind the stadium towards the track that led high up to the left of the sanctuary behind the present village of Delphi. One of the youths played the part of Bacchos. Wreathed with garlands of ivy and vine leaves, and playing his shrill double flute, he ran upwards over the high steps of the theatre, and at his passing the Thyiads followed, running and leaping, shouting 'Evohi. Oh, Bromius comes.' The lights from the torches, like flickering stars, marked the path of the ecstatic band as they climbed the mountain, high up in the darkness. In the *Antigone*, Bacchos is summoned by the words: 'Thou that leadest the dance of the fiery stars, lord of the voices of the night, Zeus-born child, Appear Lord, with thine attendant Thyiads, who all night in frenzied ecstasy dance; Iacchos our Master.'

In the quiet night when the sounds are magnified and distorted, as they echo from the mountain side, the cries and the singing and the beat of drums would be heard long afterwards drifting down from the heights above.

At one time the ecstatic rites were supposed to have been celebrated with blood and terror. The youth who played the part of Bacchos would have been torn to pieces in reality, and his body eaten by the demented women. Intoxicated by the ecstasy of possession by the god, he would have offered himself as a willing sacrifice, and in their turn the Maenads would have become one with their god by eating his body and drinking his blood. In historical times there was no human sacrifice, but any small animals that the throng met, on their wild journey, would have been killed and eaten, as Dionysos could appear in any form of animal life.

Where the orgies were celebrated we do not know exactly, but it is possible to surmise. Pausanias said: 'It is a feat for an active man to scale the heights of Parnassos . . . for they are higher than the clouds, and on them the Thyiads carry on their mad revels in honour of Dionysos and Apollo.

At one time the peaks of the Phaedriades which tower above

Delphi were confused with the summit of Parnassos, and it may have been somewhere above these that the rites were held. Although the mountains above Delphi are all part of the range of Parnassos, the actual high peaks are eight miles away, beyond the village of Arachova. High up above the wall of the cliffs of which the Phaedriades are part, between Delphi and Arachova, lies the meadow of Arachova, a plain two miles across and three thousand feet above sea level, separating Delphi from the twin peaks of Parnassos, towering yet another five thousand feet higher.

Above the Phaedriades, where the band of Thyiads wandered, is a region of grassy woodlands where today the shepherds live during the summer months, minding their flocks of sheep and goats, and making the cheese for which Parnassos is famous. Here is the tall conical hill, called Sarandavli, and near its summit is the entrance to the cavern of Korykia, sacred to Pan and the nymphs. Near here was once the ancient town of Lykorea, from which the Delphians were said to have come, and the shepherds of today still call the wooded slopes 'Lykorea'. It was to the 'craggy Korykian heights on Parnassos' that Euripides says the Bacchantes, or Thyiads went, and their rites were in some way connected with the cave. Nothing has changed on these high pastures, three thousand feet above the olive trees that carpet the valley below. All is silent except for the sound of the wind and the tinkling of hundreds of sheep bells, and nearly two thousand years have passed since the last echo of the shouting and singing died away.

In November when the Athenian girls joined their sisters of Delphi, the autumn had already come. Sometimes there would still be hot, sunny days, when the air tingled with the promise of frost not far away. In Delphi, sheltered in the fold of the mountain slope, summer can still seem to linger in November. Up on the steep path at night, however, as the girls climbed higher, the frost would be hard. Even in fine weather it would be bitterly cold, especially for the Athenian girls from the warmer south. In bad weather when the autumn rains were early and the thunder echoed from peak to peak across the valley, the orgy became a test of endurance, and the Thyiads would be glad to reach the shelter of the cave. The anxious watchers down below in Delphi would often fear for the safety of the girls, when snow clouds were gathering on the mountains. On one occasion, one of the shepherds came down to say that the girls were caught in a great snow storm. A rescue party was sent up the mountain and, before they found the girls, all their clothing was frozen. Another time, the Thyiads were unable to find their way down the mountain, and wandered far afield until they climbed down into the town of Amphissa, fifteen miles away. The local people found them fast asleep in the market-place next morning, exhausted from their ordeal.

The autumn orgy of Dionysos at Delphi was a terrifying example of the ecstatic enthusiasm which possessed his followers. It is hard, in these wintry surroundings, to imagine 'the maidens bearing the thyrsus, joining in the enthusiasm, worshipping the god with cries . . . forming groups to do sacrifice to the god and raving and hymning the presence of Dionysos, representing by their actions the legendary maenads who accompany the god of old', as Diodorus wrote in the first century B.C.

Among the Greeks the religious ecstasy of the festivals of Dionysos was not a product of asceticism and the wearing of hairshirts, but a relaxation of tension and a freedom from inhibitions, which led for a time to the complete abandonment of personality to the power of the god. Wine, the gift of Dionysos, played its part and his followers were often 'under the pleasant influence of Bacchos'. There was also sexual freedom, but the god did not demand promiscuity. His ecstatic followers were free to indulge their own natural desires or to show restraint.

As Euripides says in the *Bacchae*: 'Dionysos compels no woman to be chaste in love. That is a matter for her own character. She who is naturally pure of heart will take her place in the Bacchic dance without being corrupted.'

The festivals at Delphi, however, were not simply a time of indulgence and carnival merriment, as they were in other places and at other times, but they included a terrifying incursion of the forces outside the normal consciousness of men and women.

THE history of Delphi is like a kaleidoscope reflecting the brilliance of the world whose centre it was; but Delphi was also the source of much of that brilliance. It was an inspiration to the Greeks over many years and its history is longer than the history of the Greeks themselves. When their greatest glory was a thing of the past, the light of Delphi still burned, however dimly, and in the time of legend, before history began, before the Greek-speaking people arrived, we know from archaeological finds that early man regarded Delphi as sacred.

On the steep mountain slopes lonely shepherds minded their flocks, just as they do today, and with all the forces of nature, sometimes so lyrically beautiful and sometimes so terrifying and awe-inspiring, it would have been natural for these simple people to see evidence of strange gods all round them. Legends suggest that even in those early days there were mysterious powers to be found near Delphi and perhaps, in the sound of the wind, or the falling of the water, they would hear the voice of the great Mother Earth whom they worshipped. Here they would gather early in the year to celebrate their primitive festivals, and to perform the rituals to make their flocks multiply, and the corn sprout. Here, too, in gratitude for the fertility of the land, or as a suggestive persuasion, they would bring their offerings of small clay, female figures, often obviously pregnant. These little figures are found in the lowest levels of today's excavations at Delphi, just as they are found throughout the Mediterranean where stone-age man worshipped the strongly female principle of fertile Mother Earth.

The plains at the foot of Parnassos, on the edge of the Gulf of Corinth, were cultivated and small communities prospered and built villages that grew into towns. The oldest town of all was the port of Kirra, at the mouth of Pleistos, near the modern town of Itea. Kirra is so old that as far back as Roman times, when there was a flourishing harbour there, it had been in existence for over two thousand years. The capital of the region was a town called Krissos, which was built on a spur of rock near Delphi, and although it is only a small village now, it was then of some importance and from it the whole district was later known as 'the land of Krissos'.

Very little is known about the people who lived there at first, but we do know that with the great migration from central Europe and the north, there came invasions of Greek-speaking people between 2000 and 1400 B.C. Throughout Greece and even farther, beyond the Mediterranean, the kingdoms of the Achaeans were founded. The 'long-haired soldiers of Achaea' described by Homer, were proud feudal lords, and the greatest of them all, the leaders of their culture, were the rulers of Mycenae 'rich in gold'.

This period, known as Mycenaean, was influenced by the even more ancient civilization of the Minoans in Crete, and it developed as a uniform culture throughout the Eastern Mediterranean.

The Mycenaeans built their houses in Delphi and possibly, if Homer is to be believed, respected the powers of divination that existed there. 'Rocky Pytho', as he called Delphi, became widely known as the oracle, or a place where the gods spoke.

About 1200 B.C. there were invasions from the north by yet another Greek-speaking people. These were the Dorians, fierce fighting men, ancestors of the Spartans who believed that they were the sons of Herakles, the mighty hero of Greek legend. They were not a highly agricultural race, but irresistible in battle, and one by one the great Mycenaean centres were destroyed and the massive fortifications left in ruins. The Mycenaean culture was based on a highly organized central authority, and many of their carefully kept records have been found in the remains of their splendid palaces, on the soft clay tablets, which were preserved by the fires of the invaders. With the defeat of the central authority, the unity of the Mycenaean culture came to an end. There were mass migrations from many parts of Greece, and centre after centre was depopulated. Following their victorious armies, other Dorians came to settle in the rich lands they had conquered, and some of them stayed in Delphi, bringing to the home of the oracle new ideas and strange gods.

After the Mycenaean Age, there came a time about which little is known, as the old craftsmen had fled, and the early Dorians left little of their handiwork for archaeologists to discover. Then, at last, signs of a new culture started to appear.

The most durable trace of an early culture is to be found in the pottery that was produced. Most remains of a people corrode or, if they are valuable, are stolen, but broken pots are thrown away, and sometimes even preserved whole ones are found, from which archaeologists can date and reconstruct much of the life of a forgotten era.

New designs of pottery were produced about a hundred years after the coming of the Dorians. At first there was a rather crude, simple pottery known as sub-Mycenaean, which was followed by a type known as Geometric, because of its painted patterns. This beautiful pottery, first produced in the Ionic country around Athens, was the earliest sign of the beginning of a culture which was to reach its peak five hundred years later.

In Delphi towards the end of the Geometric Period, there was great activity and a new type of votive offering replaced the old female figurine of Mother Earth. This was in the form of a young man; a god had taken the place of the old goddess. These new virile figures were not only brought to Delphi, but were actually made in the sanctuary.

Travellers coming through the mountain pass brought the news that at Delphi a new and powerful voice was to be heard giving authoritative answers to questions of all kinds and advice that appeared remarkably sagacious. Stories of the success of the oracle were told even in remote parts of the barbarian world, often, no doubt, exaggerated as they passed from person to person, but the rulers of far-off kingdoms decided to test the powers of this oracle for themselves.

With its increasing fame, more and more people settled round the shrine. Enterprising craftsmen, and other small tradesmen soon took advantage of the stream of visitors to the oracle, as they always have done in similar circumstances. There was, no doubt, a brisk sale of images and religious articles which, as time went on, became more beautiful and elaborate. As well as bronze statuettes, all kinds of other articles were made, the most important of these were the tripods —the three-legged stands and urns, often finely ornamented.

Pottery in the form of vases of all kinds was made locally and was brought by visitors from other places, coming by land and sea from all parts of the known world; the identifying of this pottery has helped archaeologists enormously in assessing the growth of importance of Delphi at that time.

A sacred area near the spring at the foot of the Phaedriades had already been enclosed and now it was enlarged and the first stone temple of Apollo was erected. This was the same temple that we know was destroyed by fire many years later, in 548 B.C., but legends say that it was the fourth to stand on the same site. Pausanias was told when he visited Delphi that the first temple was made from laurel boughs and resembled a hut, and the second was 'built of the wax and wings of bees'. The third temple was made of bronze and it was said that there were golden song-birds on its roof, and that this temple was made for Apollo by Hephaestos, the god of metal-working, but the cautious Pausanias, visiting Delphi in Roman times, said it was no marvel that the temple should be made of bronze as: 'The Romans have a forum remarkable for its size and magnificence with a brazen roof. So that the Temple of Apollo should be brazen is not improbable. In other respects however I do not accept the legend about the temple being by Hephaestos, or about the golden songsters.'

There was another tradition that one of the earliest temples was built by a priest called Pteras and here there was a connection with Crete, as the city of Apteraei in Crete was also named after him. It was always thought that among the earliest priests of Apollo there were Cretans, who were at that time considered to be authorities on religious matters.

Year by year Apollo at Delphi became steadily more wealthy and famous. It was a special feature of the growth of Delphi that its influence should have spread so widely, and no other cult ever achieved such universal appeal as the oracle of Pythian Apollo.

Among the visitors to Delphi were the Etruscans, also called the Tyrrhenians, who after the Phoenicians became the greatest sailors of the ancient world. The ancient Greeks regarded them as pirates and often told tales of their raids and attacks on ships. The Etruscans were a superstitious people and always wanted to find out what the gods had in store for them. They might well have been attracted to the oracle of Delphi, and we do know that at some time they adopted the worship of Apollo, giving him the name of Aplu or Apulu and setting him among their other gods. From the visits of sailors like the Etruscans and travellers of all kinds, the priests of Delphic Apollo probably learnt a great deal of the outside world.

The years 750–600 B.C. were the period of greatest colonization by the Greek cities. It was at this time that Delphi rose to its position of importance as the centre of the whole Greek-speaking world, a position which it retained throughout most of its long history.

Either through the increase in population in a country that, even in those days, found it difficult to produce adequate food crops, or through political pressure, many Greek cities sent chosen people with their leaders to set up new cities in distant parts of the known world. They were not colonies in the modern sense, but independent states that at the same time had special sentimental bonds and loyalties to their parent cities. In addition they had a special link with Delphi. Before trying to establish a colony, the Greeks usually went to Delphi to get advice from the oracle. It was a wise precaution to get divine protection before setting out to face the dangers of the unknown lands, but there was also a very practical reason. The fame of Delphi had spread throughout the known world, and barbarians as well as Greeks came to consult the oracle, so the priests often knew what things were like in other parts of the world and whether they were suitable for colonization. Through successful oracles they would also have gained political influence invaluable to the colonizers. The blessing of Apollo was very desirable for a new venture, but there was also some very expert advice to go with it, when you went to Delphi.

All round the Mediterranean and far into the Black Sea Greek towns were founded. Even today, Greek names are scattered along the coasts of Italy, France and Spain. Naples is Neapolis—'New Town', Reggio is Rhegion—'the rent', because of the narrow strait. Syracuse and Gela, smaller than they once were, still exist in Sicily. Monaco got its name from a shrine of Herakles Monoikos—'Herakles who dwells alone'. Antibes is Antipolis—'the city opposite'. Nice is Nike—'Victory'; Agde is Agathe—'the good place' and Marseilles was once the Greek city of Massilia. All round the coast of what is now Byzantium, and into the Black Sea, there were Ionian Greek settlements that later came under the rule of the Lydian and Persian kings. Ionian dedications from these parts were always a prominent feature of the Delphic treasury. The little oracle had become famous, from Spain to the end of the Black Sea.

Over the years the original colonies grew and became rich, but they never forgot the debt they owed to Apollo at Delphi. He had advised their founders about which direction to take in order to find a new land which would be blessed by the gods. In return they sent gifts to Delphi, no longer simply as colonials, but as proud citizens of wealthy new communities. Their strong attachment to Delphi made them look to it always as a 'common meeting-place'.

It was not only the Greeks who sent gifts to Delphi; barbarians as well poured riches on her. Herodotus tells the story of Gyges, who was one of the first barbarian kings to send great gifts to Delphi.

Gyges was a bodyguard to Candaules, the king of the Lydians of a royal family which had reigned for twenty-two generations, over a period of five hundred and five years. Candaules thought his wife was the most beautiful of women, and extolled her virtues to Gyges in exaggerated terms and, eventually, he invited him to see her naked in order to prove his point. Gyges was shocked at the proposal but did not see how he could defy the king. Candaules instructed him:

I will place you behind the open door of the apartment in which we sleep; as soon as I enter, my wife will come to bed; there stands by the entrance a chair; on this she will lay her garments one by one as she takes them off, and then she will give you an opportunity to look at her at your leisure; but when she steps from the chair to the bed, and you are at her back, be careful that she does not see you as you are going out by the door.[1]

Unfortunately she did see Gyges and, the next day, she sent for him and said that if he was not to suffer an immediate death for his disgraceful behaviour he was to kill the king and so take possession of both the queen and the Lydian kingdom. Gyges

[1] Herodotus, *History*: I. 9.

H

therefore killed the king and was confirmed in his new status by the oracle at Delphi. Herodotus adds:

Gyges therefore sent many offerings to Delphi, for most of the silver offerings are his: and besides the silver he gave vast quantities of gold; and among the rest, which is especially worthy of mention, the bowls of gold, six in number, were dedicated by him . . . and thirty talents in weight. This Gyges is the first barbarian whom we know of that dedicated offerings at Delphi; except Midas . . . for Midas dedicated the royal throne on which he used to sit to administer justice, a piece of workmanship deserving admiration.[1]

The names of these benefactors have come down to us today as symbols of great wealth. Even more famous for his wealth than Midas, was Croesus. Croesus was the great great grandson of Gyges, and his father had given Delphi a large silver bowl, on an inlaid iron tray. After Croesus had tested the powers of the oracle, he lavished wealth on the god. It was:

. . . his own property, the fruits of his patrimonial riches [that he gave]. . . . He offered three thousand head of cattle of every kind fit for sacrifice, and having heaped up a great pile, he burnt on it beds of gold and silver, vials of gold, and robes of purple and garments. . . . When the sacrifice was ended, having melted down a vast quantity of gold he cast bricks from it; of which the longest were six palms in length, the shortest three, and in thickness one palm: their number one hundred and seventeen; four of these, of pure gold, weighed each two talents and a half, the other half-bricks of pale gold weighed two talents each. He also made the figure of a lion of fine gold weighing ten talents. Croesus, having finished these things sent them to Delphi, and with them these following; two large bowls, one of gold and the other of silver. . . .

So the list goes on, ending with . . . 'the statue of a woman in gold three cubits high, which the Delphians say is the image of Croesus's baking woman; and to all these things he added the necklaces and girdles of his wife'.[2]

It appears that the Delphians had a sense of humour, even when overwhelmed by the lavish gifts of a barbarian. The

[1] Herodotus. *History*, I. 14.
[2] Ibid. 1. 50.

strong sense of individual freedom, which was so characteristic
of Greek thought, made the despotic and sometimes irrational
behaviour of the rulers of Asia Minor appear fantastic. Centuries later, it was the laughter of his Greek soldiers that so
enraged Alexander, when he told them to bow down and
worship him in the way the Persians were so willing to do.
Usually the Greeks concealed their amusement or contempt
when they saw that there was so much wealth for the temple to
be gained from the generosity of barbarian kings.

Before 600 B.C. the history of Delphi can only be seen
obscurely through legend and tradition, and by indirect refer-
ences, but after this date there are numerous texts which
archaeologists confirm by their excavations, and the true history
starts from about that time.

Some forty years before Croesus enriched the treasuries at
Delphi, a major event had taken place which marked the turning point in Delphic affairs. It was the First Sacred War,
596–590 B.C.

Although foreign rulers brought wealth to Delphi, the
Greeks also came in increasing numbers. They came from every
part of the mainland, from the distant colonized settlements as
well as from the scattered islands, to consult the oracle and pay
homage to Apollo at the temple.

Delphi was then part of the territory of the Phokians at
Krissos, who exploited the flow of visitors and controlled
Delphi ruthlessly and greedily. The priests did not like to see
powerful Krissans taxing visitors to the sanctuary and so
depriving the oracle of some of its revenue. They protested that
this was impious, and appealed to other states to help free the
god. For a long time the leaders of the more powerful Greek
cities had felt that Delphi was a special sanctuary of all the
Greek people, and that it should not be used for the benefit of
one particular region. At that time Solon, who later formulated
the laws on which democracy was founded, was a leader in
Athens. According to Plutarch:

Solon was much honoured and esteemed, for the oration he made in
defence of the temple of Apollo, in the city of Delphes: declaring that
it was not meet to be suffered that the Khirraeans should at their
pleasure abuse the sanctuary of the Oracle, and that they should aid
the Delphians in honour and reverance of Apollo. Whereupon the

council of the Amphictyons, being moved with his words and per-suasions, proclaimed war against the Khirraeans.[1]

This action later became known as the First Sacred War.

The Amphictyons were originally a group of people united for the common performance of religious duties. They were supposed to have been founded by Deukalion, the Greek Noah, and they had their headquarters at Pylae, near Thermopylae. At the time of the First Sacred War, the Amphictyony was a league of states of Central Greece, and its principal member was Thessaly. Each of the states elected a representative to sit on the Amphictionic Council, whose duty it was to safeguard the traditions of religious ceremony, and to preserve the temples and sacred places. Like other religious foundations of more recent times, they eventually became very powerful.

The Amphictionic League was already prepared to intervene in the war; this was not entirely from religious motives as Thessaly was only too pleased to attack Krissos. Delphi was a key point on the route from Thessaly to the south and the west, and controlled all the traffic between the Gulf of Corinth and northern Greece. The Krissans imposed heavy taxes not only on pilgrims, but also on the traders from the two sides of Greece.

One of the special duties of the League was to ensure that the sacred land round Delphi remained uncultivated. It was to be used permanently as a pasture and no crops should be grown on it. This was one of the commands that came from the god himself. The people of Delphi could not become farmers but had to rely on the revenues from the temple and the oracle. Their livelihood depended on the gifts and sacrifices of the suppliants and the many profitable activities of the sanctuary. It meant that for the first time there appeared what was, in effect, a professional priesthood. This was a unique situation in Greece, where priests were usually men with other interests, and not a special caste dedicated to the life of a temple or cult.

The oracle was, of course, consulted about the impiety of the Krissan people. An action as positive as a war in defence of the rights of the sanctuary must have the sanction of Apollo. The oracle gave the answer: 'You will never take the tower of the

[1] Plutarch. *Parallel Lives*, Solon. Plutarch, like other ancient writers, confused Kirra with Krissos which were closely linked.

city and make it fall, until the waves of blue-eyed Amphitrite, thundering on the holy capes, surge against my precinct.'

There was no clear demarkation of the boundaries of the sacred land until then, and the Amphictionic League interpreted the oracle as meaning that the whole of the Krissan plain should be dedicated to the god, right down to the sea. The land occupied by the Delphians on the mountain was barren and the old ruling that all the sacred precincts should remain uncultivated imposed no new hardship, but the adding of so much fertile ground, which now came under the ban, led to many disputes, and troubled Delphi in later years.

In 590 B.C., in this First Sacred War, a united force of Greek states destroyed Krissos and 'free access and free use of the oracle was assured to all'. Delphi and her lands between the Phokian and Lokridian territories became autonomous and her independence was guaranteed by the other Greek states. These states delegated their powers to the Amphictionic League, which was charged with the duty of attending to the temporal powers of the god, to protect and avenge him.

It was recorded by Aeschines many years later, that the vows of the Amphictionic League included many moral statements, suitable to a body that was originally formed to maintain religious activities. They sought to moderate the harshness of wars, even if they had no wish to prevent them. One of the vows was that they would not cut off water from a beleaguered town; this was influenced, perhaps, by the old story that when the League attacked Krissos in the First Sacred War, they poisoned the town water-supply with hellebore and overcame the inhabitants when they were helpless. The story was probably a fiction; hellebore is not very poisonous, but as a drug was often used as a means of driving out evil spirits.

The new administration brought a resurgent energy to the life of the sanctuary. The first Pythian Games were inaugurated, and it was agreed that they should be held every four years. Very soon the celebrations at Delphi equalled those of Olympia, with the added attraction of the oracle. Building and restoration was accelerated; no less than twelve 'treasuries' were built between 590 and 550 B.C. around the old temple. These were small buildings dedicated by individual cities to contain their more valuable offerings. The treasuries were built on the lower

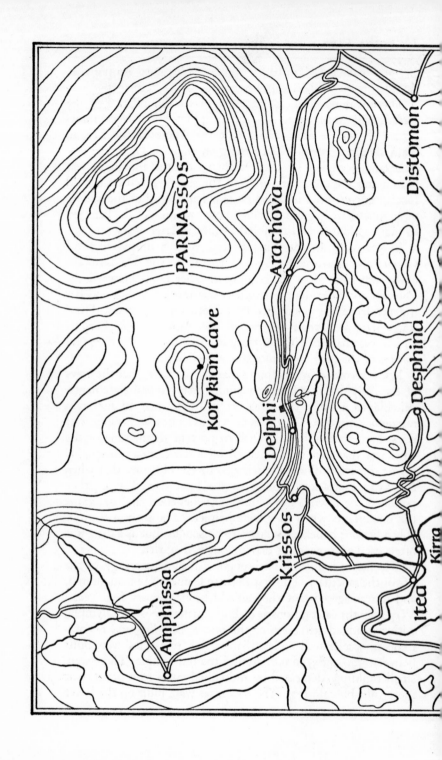

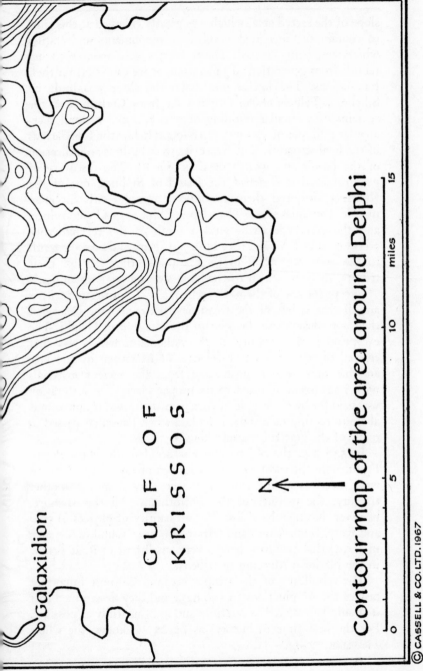

Contour map of the area around Delphi

Galaxidion

GULF OF KRISSOS

N

0   5   10   15
        miles

© CASSELL & CO. LTD. 1967

slope of the sacred area, which was greatly enlarged at this time to contain the increased number of monuments and statues which were being erected. The treasuries were maintained and rebuilt from generation to generation, as we can see from their foundations. The lowest one down the slope was built by Sikyon, a Peloponnesian city not far from Corinth, and the remains of a circular building of 580 B.C. and a small rectangular building of 560 B.C. were found below the foundations of the final structure. The treasuries were built as an indication of the power and wealth of their donors. The discovery of gold mines that enriched the island of Siphnos, one of the Kyklades, inspired them to build a temple with Siphnian marble. Pausanias says: 'The island of Siphnos had gold mines, and the god bade them send a tenth of the revenue thus accruing to Delphi, and they built a treasury and sent the tenth to the god. But when in their cupidity they left off their tribute, then the sea encroached and swept away their mines.'[1]

Except for one of them, the remains of sculptures and friezes are all that is left of the treasuries today, and the beauty of their sure design may be seen in the museum of Delphi. The exception is the treasury of the Athenians, which was first erected to commemorate the battle of Marathon in 490 B.C. and has now been reconstructed from the ancient materials with every stone restored to its proper place. The restoration was paid for by the people of Athens in 1906 and it now stands alone to remind us of how it looked when Pausanias passed so many of the graceful treasure houses.

In 548 B.C. the old temple was accidentally burnt down. Fortunately the most precious offerings of Gyges and Croesus were saved as at the time they were stored in yet another treasury, the treasury of the Corinthians. All this treasure, however, has now been lost, but a quantity of objects in gold and ivory, bronze, iron and terra-cotta, were found in a trench in 1939; this may have been a very small part of it. It is now in the National Museum in Athens.

The rebuilding of the temple became the most important task of the Amphictiony in 548 B.C., and they determined that it should be restored as carefully and as beautifully as possible. For the first time in history, as far as we know, the whole

[1] Pausanias. *Description of Greece.*

Greek world shared in sending contributions towards the building. The Delphians themselves had to supply a quarter of the required money and they travelled throughout the world asking for funds. Herodotus says: 'When the Amphictyons contracted to build the Temple that now stands at Delphi for three hundred talents, the Delphians went from city to city and solicited contributions, and doing this they brought home no small amount from Egypt. For Amasis gave them a thousand talents of alum, and the Grecians who were settled in Egypt twenty minae.'[1]

It happened that at that time Pisistratus was the tyrant, or dictator, of Athens. It was a benevolent dictatorship and the fame of Athens owed very much to him, but the Athenians, a stubborn, outspoken people, traditionally resented any form of dictatorship and inevitably many of those who opposed Pisistratus were sent into exile. Among them was the famous Alkmaeonidae family, who went to live in Delphi. In order to increase their influence, and hoping to prepare the way for their return to Athens, the Alkmaeonidae suggested that they should undertake the building of the new temple.

Thereupon the Alcmaeonidae, practising every scheme against the Pisistratidae, contracted with the Amphictyons to build the temple which is now at Delphi, but then did not exist; and as they were wealthy, and men of distinction, they constructed the temple, in a more beautiful manner than the plan required, both in the other respects and also though it was agreed that they should make it of porine stone, they built its front of Parian marble.[2]

It was customary to fine building contractors if they did not fulfil the plans, or did not use the right materials, but in the case of the great Alkmaeonidae temple, the Delphians got a better building than they expected.

To support the terrace of the temple, the tremendous polygonal wall, nearly a hundred yards long, was constructed from enormous blocks of limestone, cut with curves that fit closely to one another. On this wall official notices have been carved, and hundreds of inscriptions recording the freeing of slaves (one of the special features of Delphi) can be seen still.

[1] Herodotus. *History*: II. 180.
[2] Ibid. V. 62.

All the work on the new temple was stopped for a time when the Persians, under Darius, attacked Greece but were defeated at the battle of Marathon. Ten years later, in 480 B.C. under Xerxes, the Persians launched a full-scale invasion. According to a rather exaggerated estimate of Herodotus, Xerxes had an army of over five and a quarter million men, and for the first time the oracle seemed to lose its nerve. It gave warning of bloody calamity to the worried Greeks. Happily the advice that followed, that 'the wooden walls' would save them, was interpreted as meaning that only in their ships could the Greeks defeat the Persians; which they did at the battle of Salamis.

As the invading Persian armies advanced into Greece, the defences collapsed one by one. Many parts of the Greek world capitulated easily, or went over to the Persians, often to settle their own feuds with neighbouring states. The Thessalians sided with the Persians, and the Phokians were the only people in that region who opposed them '. . . for no other reason, as I conjecture, than their hatred of the Thessalians; but if the Thessalians had taken part with the Greeks, in my opinion the Phocians would have sided with the Persians',[1] says Herodotus.

The Persian invasion left Delphi surrounded, and part of the army marched towards the sacred shrine in order to plunder it of its treasures.

The Delphians, having heard of this, fell into great consternation, and being in a state of great terror, consulted the Oracle respecting the sacred treasures, whether they should hide them underground or transport them to another country. But the god would not suffer them to be moved; saying 'that he was able to protect his own!' The Delphians having received this answer, began to think of themselves: accordingly they sent their children and their wives across to Achaia; and the greater part of their men ascended to the tops of Parnassos and carried their effects into the Corycian cavern; whilst others withdrew to Lokrian Amphissa. Thus all the Delphians abandoned the city except only sixty men and the prophet. When the Barbarians were advanced near, and saw the temple in the distance, then the prophet, whose name was Aceratus saw the sacred arms, which it was not lawful for any man to touch, lying before the temple, having been brought out from within the fane. He therefore went to make

[1] Herodotus. History: VIII. 30.

known the prodigy to the Delphians who were at hand. But when the Barbarians, hastening their march, were near the temple of Athena Pronaea . . . thunder fell on them from heaven, and two crags broken away from Parnassos bore down on them with a loud crash, and killed many of them, and a loud cry and a war-shout issued from the temple of Pronaia. All these things being commingled together, a panic struck the Barbarians; and the Delphians, having heard that they had fled, came down after them.[1]

After this the sanctuary was left in peace. It was a wonderful story that was told about the god's defence of his temple, and it was added to by the tales of armed giants pursuing the panic-stricken Persians. How much was true, or was invented to save the face of the Delphic priests we do not know. It has been suggested, rather cynically, that the placing of the arms outside the house was a gesture of surrender or refusal to fight.

It seems very probable that the Delphians, who were intrepid mountaineers, had made their own plans for the defence of the city, and it was not simply an act of the god that the great rocks fell on the invading barbarians, but that there was some help from his followers. There have been numerous rock falls, particularly round the temple of Athena Pronaia, even in recent times, and mountaineers might well have known where to have encouraged them.

Eventually the Persians were defeated, in one of the battles that has had a decisive effect on the history of the world.

In spite of the earlier pessimism of the oracle, the prestige of Delphi remained intact. All the states who had contributed to the defeat of the barbarians were remembered in the offerings of Salamis and Plataea at the sanctuary. The memorial of Plataea was a large tripod made of gold, supported by a central bronze pillar with three entwined serpents on it. In the fourth century A.D. it was taken to Constantinople by the Emperor Constantine, and the bronze pillar remains there to this day. It if very much worn now, and passers-by seldom realize that this is all that is left of one of the greatest monuments in Delphi.

After the battle of Plataea, all the sanctuaries that were defiled by the invaders were purified, and it was ordered that all fires should be put out and relighted from the sacred fire of Delphi.

[1] Ibid. VIII. 36.

When they inquired of the Oracle . . . as to what sacrifices should be made, the Pythian god answered that they should set up an altar to Zeus the Liberator, but should not sacrifice on it until they had extinguished throughout the land the fire, which he said had been polluted by the barbarians, and had rekindled it fresh and pure from the public altar at Delphi. Accordingly the Greek commanders travelled round the territory of Plataea and compelled all those who were using fire to put it out. Meanwhile, Euchidas who promised to fetch the fire with the utmost speed, went from Plataea to Delphi. There he purified his body by sprinkling himself with holy water and was crowned with laurel. Then he took the sacred fire from the altar and set out to run back to Plataea; he arrived there before sunset having covered the 125 miles in a single day. He embraced his fellow citizens, handed them the sacred fire, and then at once collapsed and a little afterwards, died. In token of admiration the Plataeans buried him in the sanctuary of Artemis Eucliea and carved this verse in tetrameters on his tomb:

Euchidas, who ran to Delphi, came back here the self-same day.[1]

[1] Pausanias. *Description of Greece*, Phokis.

THE battles of Salamis and Plataea had a decisive effect on the history of the world. Greece united for the first time to defy the overwhelming power of Asia, with its vast armies, and halted their invasion. The small armies of the Greeks, defending democratic ideals against the tyrannical despots of the Medes and Persians, prevented Europe from becoming part of the Persian Empire. Such a victory by a small nation, was regarded by both sides, as only being possible through the intervention of the gods.

Aeschylus, the Athenian playwright, who fought bravely in both battles, in one of which his brother was killed, saw the rise of Greece to its pinnacle of achievement. He described the coming of 'an age of brighter glory', when the new young gods heralded the overthrow of old dark forces, in the *Eumenides*. In this play Orestes comes to Delphi to seek sanctuary with Apollo, pursued by the Furies. Apollo and Athene speak on his behalf at his trial held at the Areopagus in Athens, and defy the power of the ancient laws of blood vengeance and feud. Apollo says:

> To you Athen's mighty council, I come,
> For justice will I plead, even I,
> The prophet-god, nor cheat you by one word.
> For never spake I from my prophet seat
> One word, of man, of woman, or of state,
> Save what the Father of Olympian gods
> Commanded unto me. . . .
> I too would warn you, fear mine oracles.
> From Zeus they are.

Athene and Apollo reasoned with the Furies until, under their powerful influence the Furies changed, and became the Eumenides, the blessed spirits, heralding a new age for Greece. They prophesied:

113

The thirsty dust, shall never more
Suck up the darkly streaming gore
Of civil broils, shed out in wrath,
And vengeance, crying for death!
But man with man, and state
With state, shall vow
The pledge of common hate
And common friendship.[1]

A few years later, all the brave promise of the time when the whole of Greece was united against a common enemy was forgotten. The disputes of various factions were renewed with increased venom, but all the time the Greeks were fighting and quarrelling among themselves, Delphi continued to hold its place high in their esteem.

On one occasion in 448 B.C., the Phokians again occupied the Delphic lands, were ejected by the Spartans, but later re-established by the Athenians. This was called the Second Sacred War, but was of little consequence and did not change or destroy anything in the sanctuary.

It was during this century that the war between Athens and Sparta took place. Thucydides, the Athenian historian of the war years, describes it as the first really great war in history, as every part of the Greek world was involved on one side or the other.

After the superb age of Classical Greece, the age when the Parthenon was built, and the possibility of man's achievements seemed infinite, the bitter dispute between the Greeks heralded a decline in all their values. Thucydides described the situation which has so many unhappy parallels with our present time.

In times of peace and prosperity, cities and individuals alike follow higher standards, because they are not forced into a situation where they have to do what they do not want to do. . . . What used to be described as a thoughtless act of aggression was now regarded as the courage one would expect to find in a party member; to think of the future and wait was merely another way of saying one was a coward; and any idea of moderation was just an attempt to disguise one's unmanly character; ability to understand a question from all sides meant that one was totally unfitted for action. Fanatical enthusiasm was the mark of a real man, to plot against the enemy behind his

[1] Aeschylus. *Eumenides.* Translated by Gilbert Murray, 1925.

back was perfectly legitimate self-defence. . . . Thus neither side had any use for conscientious motives; more interest was shown in those who could produce attractive arguments to justify some disgraceful action. As for the citizens who held moderate views, they were destroyed by both the extreme parties. . . . Love of power operating through greed and through personal ambition, was the cause of all these evils.[1]

The change in the outlook of the Greeks was mirrored at Delphi in the style of the monuments. Now, more and more, there were commemorations of the fratricidal wars between Greeks and other Greeks. The monuments over which Plutarch later sighed glorified boastfully the achievements of one city against another, or told of its downfall. The bravery of soldiers, in a proclamation of victory, was used as a warning of menace to their adversaries. Right at the very entrance to the sanctuary, an Athenian at the end of the fifth century B.C. would pass in front of two monuments. On the left was the proud memorial of the battle of Marathon, an Athenian victory, with statues that were the works of the famous sculptor Phidias, but directly opposite was the monument to the Admirals; erected by the Spartans to commemorate the defeat of the Athenians in 405 B.C., it showed the Spartan admiral in the midst of his officers being crowned by Poseidon, the sea-god. The inscription triumphantly referred to the destruction of the Athenians. Thirty years later, in their turn, the Arcadians defeated the Spartans. In front of the arrogant Spartan memorial, they put up a row of bronze statues of famous heroes, and twice repeated in the inscription that they themselves, the descendants of those same heroes, had made terrible ravages on the Lakonian region of Sparta.

The war between Athens and Sparta became increasingly costly in men and materials and even more widespread. In the seventeenth year of hostilities, the Athenians sent an expedition to attack the Greek colonies of Sicily. Pausanias quotes the account that: 'When the Athenians were making preparations for the expedition to Sicily, an immense number of crows came to Delphi, and with their beaks knocked off and tore away the gold off the statues of Athene, dedicated by the Athenians . . . to deter the Athenians from the fatal expedition to Sicily.' The

[1] Thucydides. *The Peloponnesian War*. Translated by Rex Warner, 1954.

Athenian forces were defeated after a disastrous campaign and, twenty-seven years after the start of the war, the Spartans occupied Athens.

In the years that followed, although much of the brilliance of Greek thought survived, the decline of Athenian greatness marked the end of a glorious age in the history of ancient Greece.

It was in the fourth century that the worst disasters came to Delphi. In 373 B.C. there was an earthquake, floods and falls of rock, followed by fire, and the temple was once more destroyed. As in the early days, subscriptions came in from all parts of the known world. The list of subscribers mentions all kinds of people, from the King of Sparta, to the donations from the women of Sicily and the Greek islands. The plans for the rebuilding of the temple were, however, interrupted by the Third Sacred War of 360–346 B.C.

The Phokians were accused of sacrilege, probably that of cultivating part of the land set aside for the use of the temple. This was a common excuse for action by the Amphictionic League. The Amphictyons were led by the Thessalians and Thebans, who were traditional enemies of the Phokians, and they imposed a fine on the Phokians for their new impiety. The Phokians claimed that they were unjustly accused, and set up a violent resistance, against the 'champions of the god'. Athens and Sparta, allies once again, came to the aid of the Phokians. Both Athens and Sparta were bitter enemies of Thebes at that time; also they saw clearly the new danger which threatened Greece: Macedonian imperialism. Philip of Macedon was ingratiating himself with the Thessalians, and the Phokians, in making their attack, had frustrated his plans. At first the Phokians succeeded, but in doing so Delphi was fortified and the sanctuary was pillaged. The Phokians claimed that they had a special right to occupy Delphi, as they had done so before the First Sacred War, and called on the authority of Homer himself to support the tradition.

Over a period of ten years the battle continued. The Phokians were not rich people, and more and more they looked to the treasuries of Delphi to support their war-effort. At first they took money intended for the rebuilding of the temple, but later, in desperation, they melted down the offerings to Apollo, and left the most beautiful and wealthy shrine of Greece almost barren. The soldiers even dug the sacred ground and tore up the pavement of the temple itself because of a tradition that there might be buried treasure there.

Eventually they were beaten, and inevitably stories spread of the awful curses that fell on those who had committed such sacrilege. The Amphictyons declared their judgement on the people of Phokis, who were reduced to semi-servitude. Many fled abroad, and others were ordered to destroy their cities and to live in villages with not more than fifty houses in each. They were also ordered to pay an annual tribute towards the restoration of the defiled sanctuary. Worst of all, they were no longer represented on the Amphictionic Council, where Philip took their place. Before long he took precedence, and Macedonia became part of the Hellenic world.

Three hundred years later, Diodorus of Agyrium, who was an admirer of Philip, wrote:

During twenty-four years of his reign as king of Macedonia, in which he started with the slenderest resources, Philip built his own kingdom up into the greatest power in Europe. Having found Macedonia under the yoke of the Illyrians, he made her mistress of many great nations and states; and by force of personal character, he established his ascendancy over the entire Hellenic world, whose component states offered him their voluntary submission. He subdued the criminals who plundered the shrine at Delphi, and was recompensed for his championship of the Oracle by being admitted to the council of the Amphictyons.[1]

The Phokians were fined ten thousand talents, and although, finally, they only paid four hundred talents, there was plenty of money available for the rebuilding of the temple which had been delayed so long. Inscriptions record the daily cost of the experts from Athens and Corinth who came to replace the silver and gold vessels which had been melted down by the Phokians. They also state that as many blocks as possible were used from the previous temple. New porous stone was brought from Corinth and Sikyon for the building and the inscriptions show that freight rates were very high, costing ten times as

[1] Diodorus Siculus. Quoted by Arnold Toynbee in *Greek Historical Thought*, 1950.

much as the quarrying, so where possible local limestone from near Delphi was used.

Seven years later there was a Fourth Sacred War, against the Lokrians of Amphissa this time. They were accused, as usual, of exploiting part of the land of the god. Aeschines, who was the Athenian representative on the Amphictionic Council roused the Delphians to attack Amphissa. J. G. Frazer describes the effect of Aeschines' speech in vivid language.

'You see,' he cried, 'yonder plain tilled by the men of Amphissa and the potteries and cottages they have built. You see with your own eyes the fortifications of the cursed and execrated port. You know for yourselves that these men levy tolls and take money from the sacred harbour.' His words were received with a tumult of applause, and next day at dawn the men of Delphi, armed with shovels and mattocks, marched down to the plain, razed the fortifications of the port to the ground and gave the houses to the flames. It is refreshing to know that on their way back they were hotly pursued by the Amphissans, in arms, and had to run for their lives.[1]

The ill-advised action of the Athenians only precipitated the events they had feared. It gave Philip of Macedon, who was then the leader of the Amphictyons, an excuse to bring his armies against the impious ones. A year later with the help of the Phokians, now restored to grace by his clever intercession, Philip advanced into central Greece. Demosthenes, with inspiring speeches, roused the Athenian people at last. In spite of the eulogies of Diodorus, the historian, Philip did not quite find the whole of Greece rushing to welcome his 'liberating' armies. Athens made a belated alliance with Thebes, and a last desperate stand at Chaeronea in 338 B.C. They were defeated and the Theban army was completely wiped out. Philip was now the supreme leader of the Greek people. Two years later he died and his famous son, Alexander, brought new meaning to the idea of a Greek Empire by his conquest of Asia. Delphi did not profit as much as Olympia, from the triumphs of Alexander, and it was his successors who gave liberally to the oracle and increased its fame in the Greek kingdoms of the near east.

During the third century B.C. another people took control of

[1] Sir J. G. Frazer. *Pausanias and Other Greek Sketches*, 1900.

the oracle; the Aetolians. Greece was then divided into two, and the Aetolians controlled the greater part of the Greek mainland, while the Achaean League was in power in the Peloponnese. The Aetolians quite easily put down an attempt by the Spartans of the Achaean League to dislodge them from Delphi, and saved Greece from the Gaul invasion of 273 B.C.

The Gauls had raided Greece several times before, but this time the invasion turned into a full-scale war. Brennus led an army of about 170,000 men into Greece to plunder and pillage, and the Greeks rallied to protect their country, once again defending the narrow pass of Thermopylae. The Gauls were savage fighters; Pausanias says:

They fought like wild beasts with rage and fury and headlong inconsiderate valour: and, whether hacked about by swords and battle-axes, or pierced with darts and javelins, desisted not from their furious attacks until bereft of life. Some even plucked out of their wounds the weapons with which they had been wounded and hurled them back, or used them in hand to hand fight.[1]

In spite of their valour they were no match for the well-disciplined Greeks in the narrow pass, and the Gauls retired in great confusion. Later Brennus took 40,000 picked men and marched through the pass under cover of a thick fog. The Phokians who were on guard at the time, were taken by surprise, and Brennus forced his way through. He then started to march towards Delphi, hoping to plunder the great wealth there. The Delphians were very alarmed but, as before, the oracle proclaimed that Apollo would protect his own sanctuary with the words: 'The care for these things falls on me and the white maidens.' During the attack on the temple there was a heavy snow storm which might have represented the 'white maidens'. As well as snow, the Gauls suffered earthquakes and rock falls, and when the Phokians attacked them from the steep slopes of Parnassos, which they knew so well, Brennus and his men were thoroughly demoralized. Brennus was wounded and the Gauls retreated carrying their leader. As night fell they became separated and, in their panic, could not tell friend from foe and started killing each other. During the fighting the priests and priestesses came in their sacred vestments and shouted that they

[1] Pausanias. *Description of Greece*, Phokis.

had seen Apollo leaping down into the temple with his bow, and that he was aided by Athene and Artemis.

The Gauls retired, starving and harassed all the way by the Greek states. Brennus, whose wounds were not mortal, committed suicide 'by drinking neat wine freely', and none of his men got home again.

The Aetolians instituted a festival called the Saleteria to commemorate the defeat of the Gauls, which was celebrated as fervently as the old festivals, and Delphi became once again the religious capital of the Greek world, which in other respects was increasingly centred on Alexandria. Delphi was often menaced by the wars of the Aetolians against her rivals, until in 191 B.C. it was finally 'liberated' by the Romans.

At first the Romans treated Delphi with respect as the true centre of Hellenic civilization, and guaranteed its autonomy. Various cities and Greek leagues continued to erect statues to kings there, but Delphi was no longer what it had been, and its influence declined rapidly. The protection of Rome was not very effective; there was a barbarian raid on the sanctuary in 88 B.C. Even the Romans themselves began to treat the sanctuary with little respect. Sulla removed the riches and precious metal in 86 B.C. on the pretext of aiding his wars. Although he was superstitious enough to kiss a small gold statue of Apollo which he had taken from Delphi, Sulla wrote to the Amphictyons asking them to hand over the rest of the money of the temple to him, and he sent his agent, Caphis, to collect the treasures. Caphis was told that the lyre of Apollo had been heard in the sanctuary, and he wrote to Sulla informing him of this ominous sign. Sulla replied that the lyre was a sign of rejoicing and that the god was happy to give to Sulla his gold, and so the treasuries were emptied.

For a long time Delphi was neglected, although occasionally emperors made a small gesture to improve the affairs of the oracle; Domitian did some repairs to the temple but Nero, while praising the glory of Delphi, removed five hundred statues that he admired.

In the second century A.D. there was a last great renaissance. Hadrian, who loved Greece so much, lavished gifts on the sanctuary. Plutarch in those days acted with great piety as a high priest of Apollo. Pausanias visited the sanctuary and recalled all the great periods of Greek history, but he was a visitor to a museum and not a pilgrim to a shrine. The old fervour of the followers of the Pythian Apollo was gone, and the renaissance was only a last resurgence of an era that was finished.

When the proscription of paganism came in the fourth century A.D. the sanctuary had already lost all the rich offerings that had been one of the glories of the ancient world, and there were no more suppliants at the altar of the great temple.

The old city of Delphi was not entirely deserted; even if reduced to the size of a village, it was a village of some culture and importance under the Byzantine influence. The houses were made of marble from the sanctuary which was often recut with difficulty; the main street, which followed the old Sacred Way, was paved with blocks of marble from the near-by monuments; the now ruined temple acted as an inexhaustible source of material for the Byzantines; even blocks of the pavement were levered up in order to obtain the iron clamps which held them in place, and they continued to use the hot baths which the Romans had left behind.

Gradually over the course of the years, the remains of ancient Delphi vanished; even the Byzantine houses went. A few inscriptions could still be seen in the fifteenth century, when a travelling Renaissance scholar, Cyriac of Ancona, recorded some of them on his way through the ruined village. After this the sanctuary was finally buried under the earth and rock from the mountain flanks, and all knowledge of its exact position, even its name, was lost.

10 · *The Oracles of Legend and Story*

TO tourists of today, the turbulent history of Delphi and its part in the formation of the Hellenic world is often forgotten or even unknown, and the story of Apollo, like that of the other Olympian gods who were once so terrible and majestic, is relegated to the realm of fairy story and legend; but everyone still knows of Delphi as the site of an oracle. The Delphic Oracle has had a fame which even persisted when its original site was lost and forgotten.

At the time of Plutarch, the demand for the services of the oracle was declining. 'At present, there is a single prophetess and we do not grumble, for she is amply sufficient for those that want her services,'[1] he said.

Many years earlier the oracle had been a scene of tremendous activity. 'For at that time, as it so pleased God, Greece was strong in cities, and the place was thronged with people; they then used to employ two prophetesses, sitting in turn, whilst a third was appointed as assistant to them.'

The officials at Delphi had kept records of the affairs of the oracle for many hundreds of years, but it had been in existence for so long when Plutarch wrote about it in the first century A.D. that no written records existed of the earliest oracles, which were hidden in the obscure realms of legend and story.

The earliest reference to a consultation of the oracle was made by Homer in the Odyssey. He described a minstrel at the court of the Phaeacians, who sang about the occasion when Agamemnon 'was reminded of the prophecy that Phoebus Apollo had made to him in sacred Pytho when he crossed the marble threshold to consult the Oracle, in those days when almighty Zeus was conjuring up the great wave of disasters that was to overwhelm Trojans and Danaans alike'.[2]

Odysseus, when he heard the minstrel's lay, was reminded of

[1] Plutarch. *Moralia.*
[2] Homer. *Odyssey.* Translated by E. V. Riev, 1946.

122

the unhappy days of the Trojan War. Covering his head with his purple mantle, he wept. Homer probably lived about 850 B.C., and it was in the years which followed that there came the time of greatest glory for the oracle, during which it established its firm influence on the Greek people. This was when it took part in laying the very foundation of the wider Greek world; the colonization in archaic times.

Before this time of colonization, it was the custom of a state to dedicate captured slaves to the gods, or even, in times of stress, some of their own people. A state at war might dedicate a tenth of the captured enemy if they were victorious, or in times of plague or famine they might dedicate a tenth of their own population. The recipient of these tithes was usually the Pythian Apollo. In very primitive times these dedicated people may have been sacrificed to propitiate the dark gods, and so ensure the safety of the remainder. During more enlightened ages, slaves or citizens dedicated to Apollo could be disposed of as the god saw fit, and were often sent to colonize other regions in his name. It continued to be the custom to dedicate slaves to Apollo, throughout its history, and in this way they obtained their freedom, as the many inscriptions on the polygonal wall at Delphi show.

One of the legendary stories of the oracle was that of the sending of the young men and women to Crete for the Minotaur. It may have been invented by the later Athenians who did not like to think that they had been dominated by the Cretans in their past. The story was that Androgeos, the son of Minos, had been murdered near Athens, and the pollution of blood-guilt brought a plague throughout the land. The Athenians consulted the oracle, which replied, 'The end of the plague and famine will be, whenever you assign, by lot from yourselves, male and female bodies for Minos, sending them to this bright sea, as a requital for your wicked deeds. Thus will the god be appeased.'

There are many records of the peoples who were dedicated to the god at Delphi and were settled by him in a chosen place, and it became the custom to attribute almost every movement of people to the direction of the oracle. The reputation which it gained as a result added to its glory and gave publicity to its power. When, in fact, the great colonizations took place, the tradition of consulting Apollo was already in existence, and the advice of the oracle, together with the special knowledge and experience of the priests, did much to ensure the success of the ventures. Some of the replies of the oracle, preserved in tradition, show how they might have been phrased. The reply to the men of Megara when they set out to found Byzantium was: 'Happy are they who will dwell in that sacred city on the sea-girt Thracian shore and by the mouth of the Pontus where the fish and the stag graze to the very pastures. Send an expedition as quickly as possible, keeping all things in mind.'[1] As with many of the oracles of this kind, it was really intended to reassure the Megarians and bring the god's blessing on a project they had already planned in advance.

Sometimes the legends tell of how an unsuspecting person would be chosen by the god to lead a colonizing expedition. Herodotus tells the story of how the colony of Cyrenaica in Africa was founded by the people of Thera. In one version, the King of Thera came to consult the oracle on other matters, when the oracle suddenly commanded him to 'build a city in Libya. . . . But he answered, "I, O Prince, am too old and heavy to move myself, and therefore command one of these young men to do this;" and as he said these words, he pointed to Battus.' Battus was one of the citizens who accompanied the king. In another version, it was Battus himself who came to consult the oracle. Battus had an impediment in his speech. and wanted advice about it from the oracle:

For when he had reached man's estate he came to Delphi about his voice: and to his enquiries the Pythian gave the following answer: 'Battus, you are come about your voice; King Phoebus Apollo sends you to found a colony in Libya, abounding in sheep.' Battus answered as follows, 'O King, I came indeed to consult you about my voice, but you give me an answer as to other impossible things, bidding me colonise Libya: with what force?' By saying this he did not persuade the Pythian to give him any other answer; and it repeated the same response as before . . . so he returned to Thera.[2]

Battus was bewildered by the demand of the oracle, as the Therans claimed that they did not even know in what part of

[1] Herodotus. *History*: IV. 150.
[2] Ibid. IV. 155.

The Kastalian spring, whose cleansing waters are drunk
by thousands of tourists every year still influenced a
little perhaps by the awe which Delphi inspires.

The *tholos,* built by the architect
Theodorus, is one of the loveliest
parts of the sanctuary. No one
knows its use except, perhaps, to
express beauty of design.

Travellers looking for traces of the ◁
ancient city and sanctuary, saw the
rock tombs which are so numerous
in and around Delphi, tombs that
have been used and re-used for
countless years.

The Roman bath of the Kastalian
spring in which pilgrims once
bathed. The conduit is concealed
behind a stone wall, now broken,
which had a row of spouts. ▷

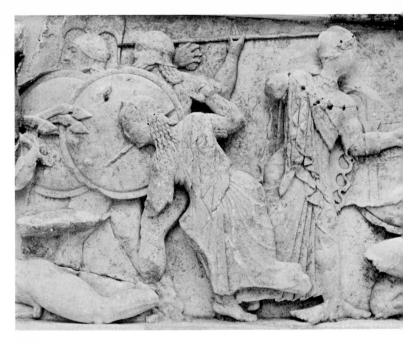

Detail of the north frieze of the Siphnian treasury. The battle
of the gods and giants (530-525 B.C.). Hera and Athene
fighting back to back; Hera is bending over to collect the
spoils of a fallen giant.

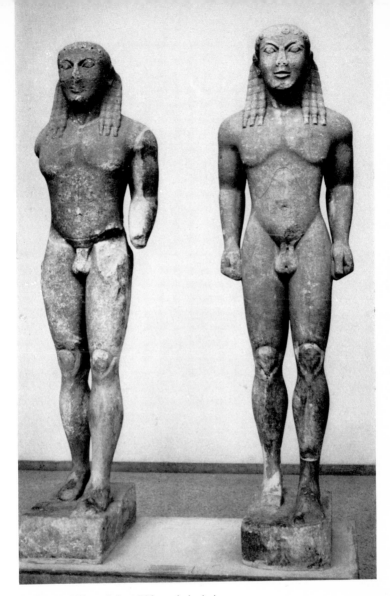

Kleobis and Biton (*circa* 590 B.C.) Archaic
statues of the two giant brothers from an
early temple. An offering from the people
of Argos.

Detail of the east frieze of the Siphnian treasury. The
assembly of the gods watching the Trojan war. The Trojan
supporters, armed Ares, Aphrodite, Artemis, and Apollo
turning to speak to his sister.

The Charioteer (475
B.C.) in all the flower
of its green-blue
patina without
corrosion, or deformity,
or fault.

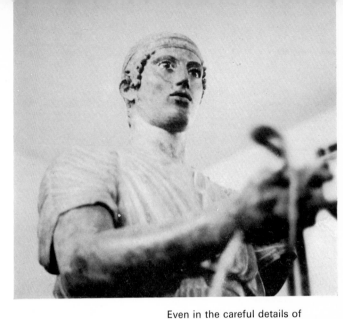

Even in the careful details of life added by the sculptor, the sure sense of incomparable artistic beauty was never lost. The long tunic is stiff and yet full of hidden movement.

The unseen threads which gather it can be sensed under the material, as it flows across the arms and shoulders.

The statue of Antinous, the favourite of Hadrian, honoured as a demi-god in Delphi to please the Emperor. The lovely texture of the Parian marble was achieved by oiling.

The Naxian Sphinx (570-560 B.C.) made from marble brought from Naxos. Once erected on a high pillar, it is now seen near the ground in the museum.

the world Libya was, and so he did nothing about the matter. Soon afterwards there were prolonged droughts and every tree except one, on the island of Thera, withered. Battus consulted the oracle again and the command was repeated, so the Therans sent him off with two fifty-oared galleys to find Libya. He was not very successful and tried to return to Thera, but the Therans refused to let such an ill-omened person land on the island again. Once more he set out and eventually he arrived at an island off the coast of Libya, but still had not found Libya itself. He stayed there with his companions for two years, during which time everything went wrong. In despair, he left one man behind on the island:

And the rest set sail for Delphi; and having come to the Oracle, they consulted it, saying that they had settled in Libya, and fared no better since they had settled there. But the Pythian gave them the following answer: 'If you, who have never been there, know Libya abounding in sheep, better than I who have been there, I very much admire your wisdom.' When Battus and his companions heard this, they sailed back again; for the god did not release them from founding the colony, until they had come to Libya itself.[1]

Here it did seem that the priests of Delphi had considerable knowledge of what things were like in Libya. The oracle continued to guide the new colony of Cyrenaica, as it was called, and in later years encouraged other Greeks to join them, proclaiming: 'He who shall come too late to lovely Libya, when the land is divided, shall hereafter one day repent.'[2] As they had been promised, Cyrenaica grew and prospered; and Battus lost his speech impediment when, 'he chanced to see a lion and his terror at the sight made him cry out loud and clearly'.[3]

With so much guidance given by the oracle, it was understandable that one of the duties of the new colony was to pay their respects to Apollo who had helped them. This took the form not only of sending gifts to Delphi, but also of honouring Apollo in their new country. Even when no legends exist of oracular guidance, it is significant that most of the early colonies had a special place for Apollo in their worship.

[1] Ibid. IV. 157.
[2] Ibid. IV. 159.
[3] Pausanias. *Description of Greece*. But cf. Pindar: *Pythian Ode*, V, where the lions were even more frightened by the foreign accent of Battus.

A great many of the stories of the utterances of the Pythia were probably invented by people to account for the founding of their own cities, and helped to add a seal of Delphic approval to their history. Some of the folk-tales were quite humorous, as was the one about Lokrus. He was told to build a city, 'where he was bitten by a wooden dog'. He pricked his foot on a thorn of a plant known locally as 'dog-bush' and decided that here was the place for the new city. It is said that Ephesus was founded by a people who were told that a fish would point the way and a wild boar lead them. The future colonists were bewildered by the advice, but set off in their ships hoping for a sign from the god. One day when they had been fishing, they landed in order to cook their meal. The food was grilling over the fire when one of the fish leapt off the coals, setting fire to a quiver lying near by. The fire spread to a thicket in which a wild boar was hiding. When the boar sprang out in alarm, the men chased it up the hill and killed it. They then realized that the oracle had pointed to this spot and so they settled in what was to become the great city of Ephesus.

In later years, long after the time of colonization, the sanctuary of Apollo became still more rich. One of the most famous stories of the oracle tells how Croesus came to lavish such great wealth on Delphi.

Croesus was the king of Lydia, which was the most powerful nation in Asia Minor at the time. The old Greek colonies of Ionia came under his rule and he knew the Greek peoples well. Solon, the law-giver of Athens, once paid a visit to the court of Croesus and had a memorable conversation with him. Croesus boasted about the great wealth of his court, but Solon refused to accept the idea that a man was greater or happier because he was rich. Although Croesus was indignant at the slight, he was probably impressed by the wisdom and dignity of the Athenian.

At that time the Persians were beginning to become powerful and Croesus was anxious to know whether he should make war on them. He decided that the best way to get advice on the matter was by consulting an oracle:

After he had formed this purpose, he determined to make trial as well of the oracles in Greece as that in Libya: and sent different persons to different places . . . designing to make trial of what the Oracle knew;

in order that if they should be found to know the truth he might send a second time to inquire whether he should venture to make war on the Persians.[1]

To test the oracles he gave instructions to his messengers to ask what the king was doing, exactly a hundred days after they had left his court, and to bring the answer back in writing:

No sooner had the Lydians entered the temple of Delphi to consult the god, and asked the question enjoined them, than the Pythian thus spoke in hexameter verse: 'I know the number of the sands, and the measure of the sea; I understand the dumb, and hear him that does not speak; the savour of the hard-shelled tortoise boiled in brass with the flesh of lamb strikes on my senses; brass is laid beneath it, and brass is put over it.' The Lydians, having written down this answer of the Pythian, returned to Sardis. And when the rest who had been sent to other places arrived bringing their answers, Croesus, having opened each of them examined their contents, but none of them pleased him. When, however, he heard that from Delphi, he immediately adored it, being convinced that the Oracle at Delphi alone was a real oracle, because it had discovered what he had done. For . . . having thought of what it was impossible to guess at, he cut up a tortoise and a lamb, and boiled them himself together in a brazen cauldron, and put on it a cover of brass.[2]

As the result of his test, as we know, Croesus lavished presents on the sanctuary.

The strange gift of second sight, which was so evident in the unimportant sayings of the oracle, left a profound impression on the thousands who later flocked to consult it, but in the oracles which dealt with affairs of men, there remained an ambiguity, which led to the name often applied to the Pythian Apollo—the Obscure. It seemed that the questioners accepted the fact that there was no certainty in the devious activities of humans.

The oracles were not merely fortune-telling or forecasting the future. It would be impious and vain to attempt to know absolutely what would happen tomorrow. Only Zeus could know what the future held in its entirety. Apollo with his clear

[1] Herodotus. *History*: I. 46.
[2] Ibid. I. 47.

vision, sharper than any human eye, could see what the results of human activity might be. He could see whether actions were good or evil, whether they were pleasing or not to the gods, or whether the gods were intending to punish or commend their followers. He could encourage the making of good laws and at other times suggest, often only with a veiled hint, that the results of what appeared to be good acts could have evil consequences.

The Greeks realized that the questions put to the oracle had to be put carefully, and that the answers had to be interpreted with regard to the frailty of the human mouth-piece through which they came. Nevertheless they wanted to be certain that nothing was left undone to prepare them for the chances of life, and to make sure, as far as possible, that they did not contravene the divine plan of things, even inadvertently.

The ambiguity of the oracle is well shown in the reply Croesus obtained when he finally consulted it as to whether he should make war on the Persians. To his inquiry the oracle replied: '. . . If Croesus should make war on the Persians, he would destroy a mighty empire.'[1] Croesus was so pleased with this answer that after inquiring as to the number of inhabitants of Delphi he presented each of them with two staters of gold. In return for which the Delphians gave the Lydians the privilege of being made citizens of Delphi at any future time, should they desire it. They also gave them the right to consult the oracle before any of the other inquirers and also allowed them to 'sit in the front seat of their temple'.

In due course Croesus was defeated by Cyrus the Persian and was condemned to being burnt alive. The story goes on to say that Croesus, in his distress, remembered Solon and called his name aloud. When Cyrus heard him . . .

He commanded his interpreters to ask Croesus who it was he called upon . . . who being constrained to speak said, 'I named the man whose discourses I more desire all tyrants might hear, than to be the possessor of the greatest riches.' Cyrus was interested in the story of Solon and wished to save Croesus, but by now the pyre was alight. Everybody tried to put the fire out, but it was blazing up more and more fiercely. Croesus, with tears, called on Apollo to save him and, on a sudden, clouds were seen gathering in the air which before was

[1] Herodotus. *History*: I. 53.

serene, and at that a violent storm burst forth and vehement rain fell and extinguished the flames.[1]

Croesus and Cyrus became friends after this. Croesus was still puzzled about the oracle he had originally received before attacking the Persians, and so he sent certain Lydians to Delphi with his fetters and ordered them to lay them at the entrance to the temple and to ask the god if he were not ashamed to have encouraged him, by his oracles, to make war on the Persians. The oracle answered:

The god himself cannot avoid the decrees of fate. . . . Croesus has no right to complain, for Apollo foretold him that if he made war on the Persians, he would subvert a great empire; and had he desired to be truly informed, he ought to have sent again to enquire, whether his own or that of Cyrus was meant. But since he neither understood the Oracle, nor inquired again let him lay the blame on himself.[2]

The priests of Delphi were in a difficult position, because it seemed that Apollo could not help but favour Croesus, after his generosity and obvious devotion to the god. The explanation came in another oracle, claiming that all his troubles were due to an ancient curse that lay on the family of Croesus, through the murder committed by one of his ancestors.

Later in historical times, the Greeks were sometimes sceptical about the oracular responses, such as the one given to Croesus, but they could not doubt that he had lavished presents on Delphi. The gifts which filled the treasuries were tangible evidence to the Greeks of the success of those early oracles and the gratitude of the consultants. The words of oracles were often exaggerated or invented to fit the circumstances, long after they had occurred, but the wealth of Delphi demonstrated the fact that, whatever form the responses had taken, they had apparently served their purpose.

[1] Ibid. I. 86.
[2] Ibid. I. 91.

LOOKING back at some of the records we have of the oracle, it seems incredible that a rational people like the Greeks should have continued to respect it and venerate it over so many years. During the historical period it was evident that the oracle was often corrupt. It cynically accepted gifts and conciliated whoever was in power. Its weakness was manifest to everyone, yet the Romans, who followed at a time when the old oracular powers were decaying, continued to venerate the powers of the Pythia. Even the Christians did not deny the power of the oracle, but by then superstition and corruption had debased the old pagan beliefs. Early Christians had reason enough to condemn the dark forces that they saw around them, but a respect for Delphi still lingered, which could not be explained away. When at last they came to look more tolerantly on the old days they suggested that perhaps the oracle had foretold the coming of its own conqueror, and the beautiful Delphic Sibyl of Michelangelo in the Vatican is a tribute to this belief.

We have to look more deeply into the place that Delphi played in the life of the Hellenistic world to understand why, in spite of its obvious weaknesses, it was still regarded as the supreme sanctuary of all Greek life.

One important thing to realize is that Delphi was the home of a god, and as such had a sanctity in its own right. The god, Apollo, represented all the desires of men to live a better, more worthy life, and we can only view with respect the little that we know of his doctrines as they evolved. A priest of Apollo, in the old stories, was often a mediator and would appeal to reason above the passions of angry men. This wisdom was set out for men to see in the sayings carved at the entrance to the temple: 'Know Thyself' and 'Nothing Too Much'. The first statement is the more famous and was regarded as the essence of the wisdom of Apollo, perhaps once spoken by the oracle. It is recorded that many other precepts, less famous than these,

were carved on different parts of the temple. All of them con-
veyed the spirit for which Apollo stood. Among them were:
'Curb Thy Spirit'; 'Keep a Reverent Tongue'; 'Observe the
Limit'; 'Glory Not in Strength' and 'Keep Woman under
Rule'.

In its dealing with countless individual inquiries, the oracle
no doubt gave sound advice and help, but the moderation and
good sense it preached to individuals it seldom managed to
bring to states and cities. On many occasions it was the direct
cause of trouble and upheaval in the political world. It was a
strange facet of the Greek mind that they could use the oracle
for their own ends without losing their faith in its ultimate
purpose.

Part of the strength of the oracle lay in its long history.
There is a sanctity that we can feel in the very stones of a
cathedral that has been used for worship for a thousand years,
and Delphi was a great religious centre for almost twice as long.
There was a sense of permanence about a place which changed
so little. Certainly from the sixth century B.C. right to the end
of paganism, nothing was really changed in the arrangements of
the sanctuary. There were cataclysms of nature, fire and earthquake and always the menace of the rock falling from the
mountainsides, but every time there was destruction the buildings were reverently restored or rebuilt in their original pattern.
The wars of men came and went; the temple was plundered,
but always new gifts came to replace the old. The sanctuary
even survived the conquest of Greece herself.

Delphi became so firmly entrenched as the centre of the
Hellenic nation, that every state venerated it. When they consulted the oracle on political matters they did, however, make
sure that their intentions were backed by well-armed men. The
oracle wavered more and more, seeking always to be on the
winning side, and becoming more ambiguous in an attempt to
evade issues. In fairness to the oracle and the Delphic priests,
the interminable disputes of Greek state against state often
made a straightforward decision impossible.

On one occasion there was a great scandal which to some
extent lowered the prestige of Delphi. The Alkmaeonid family,
who were in exile, were continually seeking ways to overthrow
the despot, Pisistratus or his son, Hippias, who at that time

was in power in Athens. The Alkmaeonidae decided that only the power of the Spartans could help them succeed. Herodotus tells the story that: 'These men, while staying at Delphi, prevailed on the Pythian by money, when any Spartans should come thither to consult the Oracle . . . to propose to them to liberate Athens from servitude.'

The continued cry of 'Athens must be freed' eventually persuaded the Spartans '. . . to expel the Pisistratidae from Athens, though they were particularly united to them by the ties of friendship, for they considered their duty to the god more obligatory than their duty to men'.[1]

The Greeks were shocked to discover what had happened, especially the Spartans, who had been duped. They did not lose faith in the oracle, however, or cast any blame on Apollo, but inevitably it was realized that the power of the oracle could be misused by impious men to gain their own ends.

It was about this time that the Alkmaeonid family built the temple of Apollo, probably completing it after their return to Athens. It was suspected, unfairly, that they had misused some of the funds entrusted to them for the rebuilding to help to overthrow the Pisistratidae. In any case the beautiful work they eventually did on the temple was used to influence the priests in their favour. The scandal remained, only alleviated by the enthusiasm of the Athenians at the restoration of their democracy.

Among the utterances of the oracle, before the internal disputes of Greece led eventually to her downfall, were those made at the time of the Persian invasion. In that great moment in the history of those days Greece was faced by the invading armies of Asia. The Athenians consulted the oracle which replied with the following warning:

O wretched men, why sit ye here? Fly to the ends of the earth, leaving your houses and the lofty summits of your wheel shaped city. For neither does the head remain firm nor the body, nor the lowest feet nor the hands, nor aught of the middle left, but they are all fallen to ruin. For the fires and swift Ares driving the Syrian chariot, destroys it. And he will destroy other turrets, and not yours alone; he will deliver many temples of the immortals to devouring fire, which now stand dripping with sweat, shaken with terror; and from the top-

[1] Herodotus. *History*: V. 63.

most roofs trickles black blood, pronouncing inevitable woe. But go from the sanctuary, and infuse your minds with courage to meet misfortunes.[1]

The Athenians were not unexpectedly dismayed at this gruesome prophecy. They were advised to go to the oracle a second time as suppliants and they threatened to stay in the sanctuary until they died unless they got a more favourable answer. The answer they got was still unfavourable, and there was an extra clause which said: 'Zeus gives a wooden wall . . . to be alone impregnable, which will preserve you and your children.' There was much argument in Athens as to what this meant, but in the end Themistocles persuaded the people that it meant that safety lay in their ships. Eventually the Athenian navy defeated the Persians at Salamis, even though the whole of Athens and the surrounding country was laid waste.

In the years that followed, the oracle became less of a political force and was more and more open to abuse. During the time of the growth of power of Philip of Macedon, it unashamedly supported him, which led Demosthenes to claim that the Pythia was 'Philipizing'. He went on to say that the new government of Delphi was so tyrannical that if anyone dared even to mention the sacred treasuries he was hurled from the cliffs, and that if Philip could not come to the Pythian Games he sent his slaves to celebrate them on his behalf.

There is a story that when Alexander was passing through Delphi before invading Asia, at a time when it was not legal to consult the oracle, he tried to persuade the priestess to answer him, and when he attempted to drag her to the temple, she said: 'My son, you are invincible.' He replied: 'That is the only answer that I need.' Later commentators regard the story as a fiction, but Alexander was very young and handsome, and it is the kind of incident that might have occurred. It wouldn't take long for his worshipping followers to spread the story round in all seriousness. It would seem to them to be another example of his divine purpose.

After the conquest of Greece by Macedonia, particularly during Roman times, the oracle took little part in political affairs, and was often treated with scant respect by the various

[1] Ibid. VII. 140.

K

rulers of the country. There was, however, another side to the power of the oracle, an influence which never really declined until the very end. This was the special place that Delphi held in men's regard as the source of moral and religious laws. In the earlier days the oracle played an important part in the forming of civic laws, the laws the Greeks had produced from time to time, in their search for a good society and as experiments in forms of government. Apollo did not form the laws himself but gave his approval of them. The Spartans claimed that the founder of their laws was Lykurgus. The tradition said that when Lykurgus was planning the new government:

He went to the city of Delphes; where after he had sacrificed to Apollo, he consulted with him about his affairs. He returned from Apollo with this glorious title given by the Oracle of the Pythia: 'O beloved of the gods, and rather god than man.' There when he craved grace from Apollo to establish good laws in his country, it answered him 'that Apollo granted his petition, and that he should ordain the best and perfectest manner of a commonwealth that ever had or should be in the world'.[1]

Whether the tradition referred to by Plutarch is true or not, it is now usually accepted that the Spartans submitted their laws to Delphi for its approval. The Spartan laws were famous for their extreme harshness in some respects. A baby boy was judged by the elders, and if he was 'deformed, misshapen or lean or pale, they sent him to be thrown in a deep pit of water'. Boys were brought up to grow into the finest fighting men of the age, partly by the rigorous training and freedom from coddling they received when they were young. It is not often realized that at the same time the women had a freedom of action which would be startling in our day, and how much more so in an age when women were reputed to be kept so much in the background.

He willed that the maidens should harden their bodies with exercise of running, wrestling, throwing the bar, casting the dart . . . and that they by gathering strength thus by exercises, should more easily do away with the pains of child-bearing. And to take away from them their womanish daintiness and fineness, he brought up a custom, for

[1] Plutarch. *Parallel Lives*, Lykurgus.

young maids and boys to go as it were in procession, and to dance naked at solemn feasts and sacrifices . . . and though the maids did show themselves thus naked openly yet there was no dishonesty seen nor offered, but all this sport was full of play and joys, without any youthful part or wantonness: and rather carried a show of demureness, and a desire to have their best-made bodies seen and spied. Moreover, it somewhat lifted up their hearts, and made them to understand, that it was no less comely for them, in their kind of exercises to carry the bell, than it was for men in their games and exercises to carry the prize.

The marriage laws were no less advanced and designed to keep 'in both parties a still burning love'.

Unfortunately there was then, as later, the danger of misusing the oracle of Apollo.

The two kings Polydorus and Theopompus . . . did add these words to the Oracle: That if the people would not assent to any ordinance of the Senate, then should it be lawful for the kings, and the Senate to break up the council, and to frustrate all things done in the same. . . . These two kings did persuade the people, that at the very first, this addition came with the Oracle of Apollo.

The great law-maker of Athens was Solon. When he consulted the oracle it was said that the reply was:

> Sit thou at helm, as governor to steer,
> To guide our course and rule the rolling ship
> For thou shalt see full many Athenians there
> Will take thy part, and after thee will trip.

Solon always gave due credit to the approval of Apollo in his actions. The Athenian laws were milder than the Spartan ones, and designed to make a gradual change to the democracy which followed.

One of the first things that Solon did was to alter the laws about capital punishment which until then applied to all kinds of offences: 'And petty larceny, such as robbing men's hort-yards and gardens of fruit, or herbs, was as severely punished as those who had committed sacrilege or murder.'[1]

[1] Ibid. Solon.

He only retained the death penalty for murder, especially when connected with sacrilege.

A new attitude to murder was contained in the earliest traditions linked with the story of Apollo. After killing the dragon, Apollo himself had been compelled to purify himself, and the idea came that it was possible to change the harsh measures of the law which were inflicted on murderers and gave rise to long blood-feuds involving all the families. Although Orestes was saved by the eloquence of Athene and Apollo, the changing of the death sentence did not mean that there was no punishment or condemnation of the crime. He suffered madness and constant tribulation until he finally expiated his guilt.

The idea that real expiation and purification was necessary to purge blood-guilt applied not only to murderers, who were tried in the ordinary way, but to all those warlike men who killed members of their own families but were usually too powerful to be brought to judgement. Time after time, the priests at Delphi and the oracle refused to admit inquirers because of their blood-guilt, or pointed out that disasters falling on a person or nation were due to blood-guilt. In the very early days of the Dorian invasion of the country it was said that a prophet of Apollo called Kadmus, who had been sent to the Dorians, was killed by a member of their expedition, and disaster fell upon them. The oracle, when it was consulted said: 'By having slain my messenger you have stained yourself with guilt.' After this all the Dorian people regularly performed a ritual known as the Karneia, as an atonement. There is a legend that the people of Sybaris, a Greek colony whose name became synonymous for richness and self-indulgence, killed a singer at the temple of Hera during a political riot. This impiety caused a spring of blood to bubble up in the temple. The Sybarites consulted the oracle which said: 'Depart from my tripods. There is still blood on your hands. I will not give you a prophecy.' Later the colony of Sybaris was in fact destroyed. In much later days the story was told that when Nero came to consult the oracle it refused to admit him on account of his blood-guilt and referred to the murder of his mother. In his rage, it is said, Nero tried to stop the oracle by filling the sanctuary with the bodies of slaughtered men. In actual fact Nero was honoured at Delphi and he presented it with a gift of 100,000 sesterces. Stories about Nero were probably spread later by the Greeks who would have been as amazed at the antics of this Roman emperor as we are. Reading about him, however, is a different matter from having to live with him. One of the kindest acts Nero could think of for someone who had insulted him was to let him choose his own manner of death, as he did with the poet Lucan.

It is not very likely that the oracle would have insulted Nero directly. The priests were always very circumspect about powerful men who came to Delphi.

Nero's chief interest was the Pythian Games, where he was carefully allowed to win the musical competition. It was said that at Olympia, where he showed off his singing, no one was allowed to leave the stadium during his performance, and that men had to feign death in order to escape from the ordeal. At Olympia, he was so annoyed to think that anyone had won anything there before him that he ordered all the statues of other victors to be thrown in the latrines. Delphi suffered a worse fate; there he removed five hundred of the most beautiful statues and had them shipped off to Rome to adorn his palace, and they were never replaced.

To give them their due, the Delphic priests did try to spread the moral and enlightened message of Apollo, whatever their actions may have been in practice, when intimidated by armed liberators.

The moral guilt of a person was judged by his intentions rather than by his acts. There is a story that three young men were coming to consult the oracle, when they were attacked by bandits. One of them ran away, the other two remained and fought the robbers. During the fight, one young man accidentally killed his friend with his sword. The two survivors eventually came to the oracle. To the one who ran away the oracle said: 'When a friend was dying, though near at hand, you did not help. I will not give you a response. Depart from the fair shrine.' To the other the oracle said: 'You slew the comrade when defending him. The blood has not stained you; you are now purer in hands than you were before.'

The moral virtues which the Delphic priests were continually trying to teach, and the Apollonian view that the spirit and not the letter of the law was all-important are shown by two pronouncements attributed to the oracle.

Holy in spirit, stranger, come to the sanctuary of a pure divinity, when you have touched the spring of the nymphs. A tiny drop will suffice the good man. But the bad all the Ocean could not wash with his springs.

And:

The temple of the gods is opened wide to the good men and they have no need of purifications. For no stain of guilt can touch their virtue. But whoso is baneful in heart, stand aside. For washing of the body will never thoroughly clean your soul.[1]

The people of Delphi were often not guiltless themselves and their own misdeeds had to be atoned for. One tragic event is concerned with Aesop, the teller of fables. He was born about 620 B.C. and Herodotus mentions that he was once a slave. His stories became famous during his lifetime and are even quoted today. He was admired by many rulers and philosophers. Among them was Croesus, King of Lydia, who in 543 B.C. entrusted a large sum of money to Aesop, intended for the sanctuary of Delphi. For some reason he quarrelled with the Delphians; one story said that it was because he attacked the priests there by means of his special gifts as a storyteller, describing them as parasites living on the donations of gullible visitors. The Delphians, in revenge, are said to have hidden a gold cup in his baggage. After he had left and was on his return journey, he was stopped and searched. The gold cup was discovered, and he was brought back to be accused of sacrilegious theft. There was a summary trial and he was killed by being thrown from the cliffs above Delphi. Plagues and famine came to Delphi as a result, and the oracle proclaimed that an atonement must be made. The priests performed the rites, but it was necessary to find the next of kin to make personal recompense. As Aesop had been born a slave and had no children or known relatives, this was difficult. At each festival afterwards, for many years, a public announcement was made asking anyone who had any connection with Aesop to come

[1] Quoted by H. W. Parkin in *A History of the Delphic Oracle*, 1939.

forward. Herodotus tells how Iadmon happened to come to Delphi and, hearing the proclamation, remembered that Aesop had once worked for his grandfather. The Delphians paid their fine to Iadmon and the atonement was completed.

On some occasions the Pythia made oracular statements on the affairs of state which gained great publicity, but later in history Delphi had little political influence. Nevertheless, the main purpose of the oracle went on unchallenged. This was to give advice and help to the countless individuals who made the journey to inquire about their personal problems. Each year many of them walked across the mountains or came by ship to Kirra and up the winding path, especially at festival times. In every age there are people who feel that fate is against them. The athlete who breaks his leg just before the race where he might have been champion. The man who sees others less worthy promoted over his head. The unsuccessful and frustrated, the worried and puzzled, existed then as now. The Greeks had someone to turn to. Someone who would tell them, perhaps, that their fate was part of things fore-ordained that could not be changed, but more often that old curses and broken vows were holding them back, and that with care they could improve the situation. Delphi was a sanctuary in a real sense to them, a sanctuary that could change their lives. There were, of course, consultations with pompous ceremonies, but at the same time there would be many less formal, more simple questions to be put to the oracle. Often they would be phrased in simple words, requiring only an answer of yes or no, and the reply would come by the drawing of lots. It was left to the god to indicate which was the better path to take.

Even the chains of slavery were loosened at Delphi. Slaves came to be made free, to be redeemed by the god himself.

Although the great gifts of the rich and powerful could sway the oracle and make the very human priests look favourably on their wealthy, well-armed clients, the god himself made no distinction between rich and poor, according to Messelière, the French archaeologist. Great success or failure meant little to the god: the only thing that mattered was the right intention of the supplicant, the true generosity of his heart. In the inscription lists of gifts to the temple, equal care was given to the recording of the poorest offerings as it was to the greatest. There was the actor Theodorus, who gave seventy drachmas, and the stater of gold from Xenotimos, the doctor. It was said that Apollo preferred a handful of ground barley from the wallet of the poor man given piously, to the wealth of the arrogant, rich man. To men of true wisdom the worth of the Delphic Apollo was not in outward forms, and the failures of the priests did not detract from the worth of Apollo's wisdom. One of the greatest philosophers of all times, Socrates, owed much to Delphi. According to Plato, Socrates claimed that the whole character of his life had been changed by an oracular statement from the Pythia when he was young. At his trial Socrates said: 'Now gentlemen, please do not interrupt me if I seem to make an extravagant claim, for what I am going to tell you is not my own opinion, I am going to refer you to an unimpeachable authority. I shall call as witness to my wisdom (such as it is) the god at Delphi.' Socrates' boyhood friend, Chaerophon, many years earlier had asked the oracle if there was anyone wiser than Socrates, to which the Pythia had replied 'that there was no one'.

This statement of the oracle made Socrates think deeply, because a message from the god at Delphi, was no light matter:

When I heard about the Oracle's answer, I said to myself: What does the god mean? Why does he not use plain language? I am conscious that I have no claim to wisdom, great or small; so what can he mean by asserting that I am the wisest man in the world? He cannot be telling a lie; that would not be right for him. After puzzling about it for some time, I set myself at last with considerable reluctance to check the truth of it in the following way. I went to interview a man with a high reputation for wisdom, because I felt that here if anywhere, I should succeed in disproving the Oracle and pointing out to my divine authority, 'You said that I was the wisest of men, but here is a man who is wiser than I am.' Well, I gave a thorough examination to this person—I need not mention his name, but it was one of our politicians that I was studying when I had this experience—and in conversation with him I formed the impression that although in many people's opinion and especially in his own, he appeared to be wise, in fact he was not.

Socrates interviewed many people in the same way, and not unnaturally made himself very unpopular, but even though it led to his death he said: 'This duty I have accepted in obedience to God's commands given in oracles and dreams.'

He described his adventures as a pilgrimage, undertaken to establish the truth of the oracle once and for all. The conclusion he came to, was that:

Real wisdom is the property of God, and this Oracle is his way of telling us that human wisdom has little or no value. It seems to me that he is not referring literally to Socrates but has taken my name as an example as if he would say to us 'the wisest of you men is he who has realised, like Socrates, that in respect of wisdom he is really worthless'.[1]

The rest of the trial and the final moving death scene of Socrates is well known, and not part of this story, but it is interesting to see how the oracle was regarded by such men as Socrates. It was the word of god to be pondered over carefully, and not just another form of divination or soothsaying.

Plato, Socrates' greatest pupil, held Delphi in deep respect. Many years later a woman inquirer at the sanctuary was told: 'You will do well to honour Plato, the expounder of godlike glory.'

In spite of all its defects, the greatest thinkers in antiquity honoured Delphi and saw something of the force behind it, but gradually over the years its powers declined. The decline kept step with the growth of superstition and cynicism of the pagan world before the coming of Christianity. When Hadrian restored the greatness of Delphi, for a short time, there was a great increase in personal inquiry, and a revival of the glories of pomp and ceremonial, but it was a last great burst of light from a dying fire.

Hadrian asked the oracle the conventional question: 'Where was Homer born and who were his parents?' The Pythia answered in beautiful verse form:

Do you ask me of the unknown family and native land of that ambrosial Siren?
By dwelling he belongs to Ithaca, and Telemachus was his father.

[1] Plato. *The Last Days of Socrates*. Translated by Hugh Tredennick, 1955.

Giving the surprising answer that Homer was the grandson of Odysseus, which may only have been a charming bit of symbolism, to please the emperor, indicated that Homer was the spiritual heir of Odysseus and his age.

Some time after the coming of Christianity, the oracle became silent and Julian the Apostate in A.D. 362, in a last effort to restore the best pagan beliefs, sent a famous doctor, Oribasius, to see if he could revive Delphi. For the last time the Pythia spoke, in tragic, moving words to the world outside:

> Tell the King the fair-wrought house has fallen.
> No shelter has Apollo, nor sacred laurel leaves;
> The fountains now are silent; the voice is stilled.

The last temple of Apollo was plundered and torn down about thirty-six years later, in A.D. 398 by the Christian emperor, Arcadius, not to come to light again for over 1,500 years.

WHEN St Paul travelled through Greece in the first century A.D., Delphi was still a place that was loved and venerated. Before Pausanias visited the sanctuary and before Plutarch served the temple of Apollo on the slopes of Parnassos, Christian apostles had been bringing news of a new and different religion. Small groups, here and there, followed the new teaching, but not at first in very great numbers. The spread of Christianity was a slow process, but year by year its influence grew. To the tolerant Greeks, the coming of a new religious belief was not a very violent change. The nature of God was seen in a new light, but the old rituals of the pagan religions were easily adapted to worship of a different kind. St Paul's letters often reflect his disapproval of the influence of the old pagan traditions on his followers, but he had to accept the fact that while some members of a family were often converted, others remained faithful to the old ways, and there was little dispute between them. The transition was very gentle, and even today the rites and customs of the Greek Church are based on a far earlier ceremonial.

For three hundred years Christianity extended its influence. Persecution of Christians by the Jews gave way to violent persecution of them by the Romans. The Greeks humoured the eccentricities of emperors who regarded themselves and their favourites as gods, but had once laughed at the idea, like Cassander, the young cup-bearer of Alexander, who was 'brought up with the liberty of Greece'. When the barbarians reverenced Alexander as a god, he had his head knocked against the wall for laughing. According to Plutarch, 'King Alexander was so offended that, he took him by the hairs of the head with both hands, and knocked his head and the wall together.'[1]

Religious persecution was once unknown to the Greeks, but Greece was later a Roman province, and many Roman

[1] Plutarch. *Parallel Lives*, Alexander.

143

emperors showed their hatred of the gentle Christians, and what they regarded as a vile and detestable superstition of a people 'convicted of a hatred of the human race', in the words of the Roman historian, Tacitus.[1]

Eventually the wheel turned and Christianity became the official religion of the Roman Empire. The Emperor Constantine was baptized, and his soldiers carried Christian banners and emblems in place of the old pagan symbols. For a long time there had been a decline in the morals and values of ordinary people. Superstition and fear had replaced the well-ordered beliefs in pagan deities. In A.D. 363 a Roman emperor, Julian the Apostate, attempted to restore the best features of paganism as an 'adventure of the soul seeking God'. He 'dismissed the thousand hairdressers, the innumerable cooks and eunuchs of his Christian predecessors'. He tried to prevent licentious theatrical shows and said: 'Indeed if it were possible to expel such shows completely from the theatres, and give back a pure stage to Dionysos, I should certainly have attempted zealously to carry this out.'[2] His efforts were in vain and when he sent his mission to Delphi, there was in reply the last despairing message, saying that the oracle was no longer functioning. It was not by any revival of pagan worship that Europe was to emerge from its dark ages, but under the influence of the new religion of Christianity.

Although very early Christian churches sometimes showed a peaceful transition from pagan to Christian worship, and myths of the older religion were frequently shown in mosaic design side by side with Christian symbols, there were also fanatics determined to remove all traces of paganism. Temples and statues were destroyed and defaced, libraries were burnt, and many ancient philosophers were discredited, being regarded as emissaries of the devil.

Delphi had already been pillaged, but after the proscription of paganism it was destroyed, and eventually even its memory was obscured and the greatness of its past forgotten altogether.

The Byzantine Age, which followed the recognition of Christianity as a state religion, lasted for a thousand years, but the centre of the Byzantine Empire was in Constantinople.

[1] Quoted by Roderic Dunkerley in *Beyond the Gospels*, 1957.
[2] Quoted by E. Wellesz in *Byzantine Music and Hymnography*, 1961.

Mainland Greece, its early glories long past, became the prey of adventurers seeking new lands. The Norman knights, originally called eastwards by the Crusades, turned to Greece and it became a Frankish land of high chivalry. Castles with drawbridges and turrets were built, from which armoured knights rode out to joust and do battle with one another, and also with the Greek Byzantine rulers. Venetian traders occupied the coasts and islands, and in their turn built fortresses and castles. Eventually they were all overcome by the Turks, who, in the fifteenth century, transformed Greece and most of Eastern Europe into the Ottoman Empire.

During the time of great castle building, one was built near the forgotten sanctuary of Delphi, to defend the pass through the mountains. In its turn this castle was destroyed and vanished, leaving behind a memory in the name Kastri, by which the village which occupied the site of the sanctuary, was known.

A thousand years after the oracle had given its last message, a new and exciting world began to open out to the wonder of western scholars. Once again they began to discover the literature and beauty of Greece that had been hidden for so long. Men began to read ancient works, often in poor translations from Greek to Arabic, from Arabic to Latin, and they began to look for other Latin scripts and to translate them. Once again they read of Delphi as it was described by Pausanias and Plutarch. When Cyriac of Ancona, with his zest for travel, wandered through Greece betwen 1436 and 1447, it was near Parnassos that he found the inscriptions that referred to Delphi, but it was not until the end of the seventeenth century that many travellers came to Greece looking for the remains of its ancient culture. They came in search of the fabulous land where the great men had lived, who were now becoming a familiar part of the literature of scholars and authors. This was the land of Plutarch, who Shakespeare knew so well, and of Delphi which Plutarch had loved.

Among the earliest travellers who wrote about Greece were Wheeler and Spon. George Wheeler was an English gentleman, who set out to explore Greece and the Near East, inspired by his reading of classical literature. The writings of the Greek philosophers in Latin translations were by now familiar, but

Greece under the Turkish rule was an almost unknown country. Later George Wheeler became a priest and was knighted, but in 1676 he was a young man, full of the adventurous spirit that had inspired the Elizabethan travellers of the previous century. He spoke modestly of the difficulties travellers experienced in those days, but in fact there were considerable dangers, not only from the Turkish officials who were suspicious and regarded them as spies, but from thieves and brigands who flourished in the wild, mountainous country.

In the early spring of 1676 Wheeler, accompanied by Jacques Spon, an eminent French scholar from Lyons, arrived at the port of Itea. Their reception was not very favourable and Wheeler wrote indignantly, 'We were made to pay a Doller a Head for our Welcom on the Grecian Shore, by an Infidel that called himself Receivour of Customs.'[1]

The first object of the travellers was to search for the lost city of Delphi. They recognized the plain, even then planted with olive trees, as the 'happy plain of Crissa', and set out on horseback across it, with only the description of Pausanias, written one thousand, five hundred years earlier, to guide them. To begin with, they went to Amphissa, then known as Salona, but immediately recognized that it bore no resemblance to the the ancient description of Delphi. Wheeler wrote: 'We enquired of our Host whether there were no Ruins of a Town in our way between this and Livadia? He told us that there were many at Castri a village about midway: So we spoke with several Janizaries to conduct us thither.'

At first the Turkish soldiers were unwilling to accompany the party and there was murmuring amongst them about spying, but eventually it was a party of eight which set off on horseback for the journey into the mountains. 'We soon began to mount the ridges of the mountain Parnassus by a very bad rough way, South Eastwards, until we arrived in four or five hours time at Castri; which we no sooner aproached, but we concluded, that it was undoubtedly the Remainder of the famous City of Delphos.'

Wheeler's description of Delphi was remarkably clear and accurate, the impression of a geographer, without the romantic feelings for scenery which marked later writers.

[1] Sir George Wheeler. *Journeys*, 1682.

Castri, or Delphos, is situate on the South side of the Mountain Parnassus, something inclining to the west; not on the top, nor at the foot of the Mountain; for it hath a great way to the Plains of Crissa below it, and much more to the Mountain above it. The high Cliffs in sight above it from the Town seem to end in two points, whence I judged it was call'd of old Biceps Parnassus: For it hath many more tops, and much higher than these, being a very great Mountain: But these two tops seem from Delphos, hide all the rest. Between which the water falls, in great abundance after Rain and Snow, and hath worn them almost asunder. There is also a Fountain with a very plentiful source of water, continually issuing from among the Rocks just under the Separation: which by the Marble Steps descending to it, and the Niches made in the Rock for Statues above it, should be the Fountain Castalia, that so inspired the antient Poets. . . . In this Cleft, about nine or ten Yards high, is a hole; which by throwing stones into it, we found to have water in it: and on the right hand I observed some Stairs, leading up to it, cut out of the rocks; but so broken, that there was no clambering up. We judged this the Antrum Corycium, or the Grotto of the Nymphs, the Poets called by that Name.[1]

The steps leading up into the rear of the great cleft of the Kastalia are still impossible to climb, but we now know that the Korykian Cave is far above Delphi, above the 'tops' of the great cliffs of the Phaedriades.

Wheeler took the opportunity to express his views about the poets of his time. 'The water of Castalia is very good and cool; fit to quench the thirst of those hot-headed Poets, who, in their Bacchanals, spare neither God nor Man; and to whom nothing is so sacred, but they will venture to profane it.'

Wheeler and Spon explored the neighbourhood of the town and found several inscriptions which confirmed their belief that this was indeed Delphi. Below Kastri on the slope among the olive trees, they saw the old Church of St Helios, which they concluded, mistakenly, was the site of the original temple of Apollo. It was nearly two hundred years later that the actual site of the temple was identified, concealed below the houses of the village of Kastri. Kastri, in 1676, had about two hundred houses 'and those very ill built', five or six churches and a mosque. The Greek villagers were 'good people though poor', and lived a semi-feudal existence under the Turkish

[1] Ibid.

overlord, who lived at Amphissa. After years of occupation by foreign powers, they had lost all knowledge of their past. Wheeler remarks: 'It is not usual that they know anything of the History of their Country,' and was astonished to find a monk in the monastery near by who actually knew that the town was once called Delphos. The travellers showed the delighted monk an inscription on the pavement of his church, which referred to Delphi. They quite correctly identified the monastery as lying on the site of the gymnasium.

Wheeler did not want to leave Delphi without seeing something more of Parnassos, about which so much was written, and so the party climbed the steep path above the town. He wrote:

We could not pass by this Mountain, so celebrated by the Poets, without passing over it to see what beauties those really were, they so much commended in it. And therefore we took our Guide we had the Day before; who willingly offered us his service, being well acquainted with this Mountain, and a fellow naturally ingenious, as most of the Greeks are. We passed between the Stadium, and the Clefts above the Town, and presently began to mount, making many turns backwards and forward, to get a little ground in height. But I being light, made no great matter of it, chusing rather to go on foot, and have my Horse led, than to venture my Neck by a stumble. So crossing all the ways, I often had time, before my Comrades came to me, to view the Plains of Salona, and the Gulph of Lepanto below me. The way is, in some places, cut into Stairs in the Rock; which seem to me very antient.[1]

From the top of the path used so many years before by the Bacchante followers of Dionysos, Wheeler looked out over the view which, just as he says, lies spread out like a map. On the other side of the valley, the top of Mount Kirphis, now far below, looks like a plain. From here he saw the great peak of Parnassos, snow-covered, and almost above the clouds and was greatly impressed: 'For indeed I esteem this Mountain, not only the highest in all Greece; but one of the highest in all the world, and not inferior to Mount Cenis amongst the Alpes.' In fact Mount Parnassos is 8,068 feet high, lower than most of the great Alpine peaks and not much more than half the height of Mont Blanc, but the impact of the view of Parnassos,

[1] Sir George Wheeler. *Journeys.*

even to experienced travellers, has little to do with absolute heights.

In the seventeenth century most Greek people were illiterate and knew very little about their illustrious ancestors. Wheeler was not interested in restoring the freedom and dignity of the Greeks: to him the glory of Greece was a thing of the past. He wrote: 'All the world knows how famous Delphos hath been for the Oracle of Apollo there, consulted for so many Ages together. But its antient Glory is now vanished; and it remains Great, at the present only in the writings of the antients,' and for more than another hundred years it was to remain forgotten and isolated among the mountains

During the years which followed the visit of Wheeler and Spon, several travellers, inspired by an ever-increasing interest in classical times, left descriptions of the ancient remains in other parts of Greece. The great value of these accounts, especially in Athens, lay in the fact that many of the temples and monuments were then still intact. The ravages of vandals and destruction by war were soon to remove or damage many of them, and only the records of those travellers tell us how much has been lost. Delphi presented quite a different picture. Here, nature and the power of Mother Earth had already completed the destruction which men had started centuries before. No descriptions in the seventeenth century could add anything to what could be seen at Delphi a hundred years later.

A change was taking place in Greece at the beginning of the nineteenth century. After years of enslavement the Greeks were awakening. Linked with their past only by the Greek language and the Orthodox Church, they were rediscovering their heritage, and starting to fight their way back to becoming an independent nation. The poets and archaeologists of other countries began to look at Greece, not only as an interesting relic of the past, but with a burning desire to bring the past to life again.

When Byron went to Delphi in 1812, there was still little to be seen of the remains of the sanctuary.

The little village of Kastri stands partly on the site of Delphi [he wrote]. Along the path of the mountain, from Krissos, are the remains of sepulchres hewn in and from the rock; 'one' said the guide 'of a king who broke his neck hunting'. His majesty had certainly chosen

the fittest spot for such an achievement. A little above Kastri is a
cave, supposed the Pythian of immense depth; the upper part of it is
paved, and now a cowhouse. On the other side of Kastri stands a
Greek monastery: some way above which is the cleft in the rock with
a range of caverns difficult of ascent and probably leading to the
interior of the mountain, probably to the Corycian Cavern mentioned
by Pausanias. From this part descends the fountain and the 'Dews of
Castalie'.[1]

The stories of caverns we now know existed only in the
mind of a guide, combined with an ancient memory of fissures
and underground chambers, but Byron's description of Delphi
in 1812 was the impression of a poet. The situation of Delphi
and the aura of the ancient power inspired him just as it
inspired Flaubert later in the century, who wrote that here was
a 'landscape full of religious terror'. Other travellers and archaeologists, looking for traces of the ancient city and sanctuary,
saw the rock tombs which are so numerous in and around
Delphi, tombs that have been used and re-used for countless
years. The presence of the tombs and also the remains of many
early Christian churches indicated that here was a place of great
sanctity, even in Christian times. The visitors explored further,
often with Pausanias as a guide, and identified the depression
above the village, where the stadium once lay. In the cellars of
the village houses there were ancient footings and occasionally
winter storms washed the mud and debris from squared marble
blocks and sherds of carved marble. The monastery below the
stream of Kastalia showed clearly the shape of a building, later
restored as the gymnasium, and there was, of course, the
marble quarry—the Marmaria—near by.

After the liberation from the Turks in 1827, Greece was
still a wild place; exploration was difficult, and serious
excavation almost impossible. The Greek people themselves
were only just beginning to realize that once again, after so
many centuries of subservience, they were a free and independent nation, and a nation far behind the rest of Europe in
communications and development. In spite of the difficulties,
many archaeologists thought longingly of restoring Delphi
to the gaze of men and the light of the sun. It was an exciting
prospect as Delphi seemed to be the most complex archaeolo-

[1] Byron. Note to *Childe Harold*.

gical site in the whole of Greece. When the excavations were eventually started, they were not simply a rediscovery of great treasures of architecture or art, far finer examples exist in other parts of Greece, but the verification of the stories told by the ancient writers. It was known that the sanctuary, once the richest in the world, had been pillaged and the buildings destroyed. No gentle fall of ash or sand had entombed and preserved the remains of the city, but here man and nature had been at their most violent and destructive, and the hopes of finding rare treasures was not great.

To the joy of the excavators many precious finds were made, but the real excitement was the gradual revelation of the whole of the history of the Greek people and the confirmation, stone by stone, of the writings and descriptions left by the great men of Ancient Greece. Many archaeological diggings reveal the arts and lives of unknown people, and the archaeologist is trying to find out by his investigations, what those people were like. The culture of the Minoan and Mycenaean Ages was completely unknown until excavations were started, but the historical writings of men had made Delphi famous, and the stories and legends connected with it were already known. Here the excavators hoped to see for themselves the evidence of events that played such a tremendous part in the story of Ancient Greece, and to discover something of the secret of the power and strength of the oracle which had done so much to guide the development of those people.

A good many years were to pass, after Byron's visit, before excavations were to start, and the difficulties were tremendous. Individual visitors were not optimistic about the possibility of finding many of the remains in the sacred area. The French archaeologist Letronne wrote, in 1820: 'One seeks vainly for any vestige of the famous temple of Apollo, of which the site is quite unknown.'[1]

There were difficulties too of a more practical kind. In 1840 a group of German archaeologists, under Otfried Müller went to Delphi and found a corner of a great wall in the village of Kastri, and underground rooms which they thought were treasure chambers. Later these were recognized as spaces between the foundation walls of the massive buildings. At that

[1] Quoted by G. Radet in *Histoire de l'École Française d'Athènes,* 1901.

time Delphi was ruled by a village tyrant called Captain
Franco, who led a band of irregular soldiers, and terrorized the
neighbourhood. This Captain Franco confiscated the gear of
the German archaeologists and stopped any excavations. Poor
Otfried Müller contracted fever in Delphi and died shortly
afterwards, and further attempts to investigate the sanctuary
were abandoned.

It was obvious that individual initiative in exploration was
not enough in that troubled area, and classical scholars and
archaeologists throughout the world, who were eager to venture
into Greece, needed organizations equipped to co-ordinate their
work, and able to obtain official sanction and protection for
them in their research. At that time, in the middle of the
nineteenth century, it was realized that there was national
glory to be achieved by discoveries in Greece, so nation after
nation founded learned institutes and schools in Athens. The
first foreign country to obtain a foothold there was France.

When the École Française d'Athènes was founded in 1846,
there was considerable jealousy from other countries. A writer
in the British Press remarked:

'For the moment we are only able to comment that the
establishment of the French School is a political move. What
advantage can Greece possibly have from this establishment?'

But it was not long before Great Britain and the other
countries followed suit.

From the beginning, the French were particularly interested
in Delphi. The cult of Apollo, who was the god of light and
reason, appealed to the French temperament, and Delphi was
his special sanctuary. The Gauls had once come to rob and
destroy the temple, and now it seemed fitting that they should
return to restore it once again. Delphi, however, remained
intractable, in spite of the hopes of the French. Although there
was competition with other countries to have the honour of
working on one of the most dramatic sites in Greece, the
Parthenon and other monuments in Athens, Olympia, Delos
and many other places, were all excavated before Delphi.

In 1858 the great French archaeologist, Foucart, later to
become director of the French School in Athens, was preparing
to go to Syria. As there were political troubles and massacres
in that country at the time, he decided to go instead to have a

look at Kastri, where someone had spoken to him of underground chambers discovered by Müller. With his colleague, Monsieur Wescher, he spent ten days investigating the site and was appalled by the difficulties involved. He wrote to the French Academy of Sciences: 'Carriages and carts were of no use in that country; everything must be carried on the backs of men, and the workmen often come on blocks of stone so enormous that they can only be moved after many day's labour.'

In spite of the problems he returned again and again to Delphi.

There were not only physical difficulties. The sturdy mountaineers of Kastri did not view the interference of strange archaeologists with much favour. They resented the incursions of these men who had come to peer into their private rooms, tearing up the earth floors and knocking down the walls behind which sheep and goats were penned during the winter. Their ways of life had remained unchanged for generations, and traditions of hospitality that made them welcome the foreigner with open-hearted generosity were sadly shaken by the inexplicable behaviour of these visitors. The very word for stranger meant guest in their language, but the stranger did not act like a guest; he talked of destroying the village where their fathers and their fathers' fathers had lived and died. One day they would understand and glory in the fact of living in Delphi, to which so many people were to come with wonder, but then all they knew was that they might be evicted from their village, and they opposed the idea in every way they could.

In July 1862 another colleague of Foucart wrote to the school in Athens: 'Messieurs Boitte and Wescher that I had left in my last letter, at the mercy of the Delphians, who are the most wicked people in the world, have returned safe and sound. They were subject to menace and terrifying swearing. Mons. Wescher who is making a serious study of modern Greek, has added many words to his "thesaurus", in the form of expressions which are at least very novel.'

In the same year, the French government was making a great effort to purchase the land round Delphi, and Napoleon III sent warships to Itea in order to 'help the enterprise'.

It was obvious that, in order to excavate Delphi, not only

would engineering skill be required, as the site was covered by rocks and earth to a depth of many feet, but the whole village of Kastri, which occupied the centre of the site of the sanctuary, would have to be removed and rebuilt elsewhere. Foucart who was then the director of the French School in Athens, asked the French Government for an extraordinary credit of 100,000 francs, about £4,000, in order to buy the thirty houses of Kastri, and the Greek Prime Minister, Koumoundourous, agreed to give France the right to purchase and excavate Delphi. Unfortunately, five weeks later Koumoundourous was defeated, and the new Greek Government withdrew the offer. Years of negotiations and intrigue were to follow before France finally obtained the permission she sought.

In the meantime, as far as possible, the work went on in Delphi. In 1880, it was possible to excavate a small corner of the centre of the village, where, behind a derelict cottage, marble pillars could be seen on the ground. B. Haussoullier, one of the French archaeologists who every year visited Delphi, cleared the space and re-erected the pillars, and once again, after being hidden for more than a thousand years, the Portico of the Athenians appeared, with its proud inscription: 'The Athenians have dedicated this portico, with the cables and figureheads taken from their enemies at sea.' In 1888 the American archaeologist, Middleton, estimated the size and general proportions of the great platform on which the temple once stood.

Greece was a poor country. After years of exploitation and, sometimes, harsh foreign rule, her national pride and dignity had returned to her, but without the resources of money and learning that other countries had acquired in the prosperous years of the nineteenth century. It was a time when the great powers of the world were competing with one another, not only in trade, but in proclaiming the importance of their own national culture. However dedicated archaeologists were in their desire to reveal the secrets of the past, political pressure to gain new achievements for individual countries was also present. In later years Greek-born archaeologists were to contribute wholeheartedly to the wealth of excavation in Greece, and today they co-operate in what is considered a joint responsibility for preserving the remains of ancient western culture, but during the nineteenth century the Greek Government was in the unenviable position of having to bargain with richer nations for their rights to excavate on Greek soil, and were naturally anxious to obtain the best terms possible.

In Athens competition for the honour of controlling the excavations of Delphi intensified. The French were indecisive, and so the Greeks offered it to the Germans who refused, out of respect for the prior scientific rights of the French. The Greek Government then tried to establish a lottery, with the support of an Austrian bank, to raise three million francs in order to excavate the site themselves, but the scheme failed. The decision finally lay between the two contenders, France and America, which had established its own archaeological school in Athens in 1881.

In the year 1889, the Greek Government offered the excavation rights to the American School, which was at first reluctant to stand in the way of the French and felt it their duty to 'guard the rights of scientific and international courtesy'. But the following year the Director of the American School considered that there was no possibility of the rights being conferred on the French. He wrote to the United States Minister: 'I heard from an eminent French authority that the French were not likely to be in a position to undertake the excavation, even if the Greek Government gave permission.' In his report of 1890, he said: 'With regard to Delphi, I have to state that my first step was to come to a clear understanding of the French claim. I satisfied myself completely that it was right for us, under the existing circumstances to endeavour to acquire this great honour for our country and for our school.'[1]

The French School in Athens was then in a low state of morale, and full of discouragement until the new director arrived in 1891. This was Théophile Homolle, the man whose name will always be associated with the uncovering of Delphi. Like other French archaeologists, he looked on Delphi as a special preserve of the French, and echoed Flaubert when he stated: 'The site of Delphi is one of the most beautiful of Greece; it is full of mystery, grandeur and divine terror.' The members of the French School in Athens saw little hope of competing with the Americans and they claimed that certain

[1] Ninth Report of the Committee of the American School of Classical Studies at Athens.

United States capitalists had offered 'to cover Apollo with dollars', and had agreed to pay everything for the excavations, but Homolle was a determined negotiator and was not going to let the prize slip out of the hands of the French. Within a few months he had persuaded his government to make a gran of 500,000 francs, about £20,000, later increased to 750,000 francs, and by means that are not recorded he forestalled the American offer and obtained the agreement of the Greek Minister. On 25 April 1891, King George of Greece signed the document giving the French a ten-year monopoly to excavate Delphi, and the Americans relinquished their claims. The Director of the American School wrote: 'While we regret the loss of the oportunity which seemed fairly within our reach, to bring to the light of day the remains of that distinguished seat of Greek religion, yet we wish our friendly rivals, the French, the highest success.'[1]

On 10 October 1892, the first stroke of a pick-axe, on the most complex and difficult site in Greece, started the excavations and the research which, seventy-five years later, was still occupying the skill of some of France's greatest archaeologists.

[1] Tenth Report. American School at Athens.

13 · Delphi Comes to Light Again: The Archaeologists

THE excavations which started at Delphi in the autumn of 1892 were not just an interest of a learned society but a source of great national pride. The French Government, which provided the grant of money, commanded the excavations to proceed, and Théophile Homolle was honoured as 'the man who assured that the glorious privilege of excavating Delphi was given to France'. He was a superb administrator, in addition to being a fine archaeologist, and under him a team of dedicated workers spent the following ten years clearing the site and protecting it from the forces of the mountain, which always threatened it with falls of rock and torrential water.

The grant of the French Assembly made it possible to purchase all the houses of the village of Kastri, together with most of the neighbouring land. Later a new village of Delphi was built a mile away, to rehouse the villagers. A light railway was laid to remove the accumulated debris and many workmen were recruited. It was not until the following year, after the removal of many tons of rubble, that the shape of the sanctuary began to appear clearly, and from then on, day after day, more and more exciting finds were made.

In 1893, at the end of April, the Athenian treasury was uncovered. It was then a pile of marble blocks beneath the earth and stone, but later it was re-erected, and now the shining white marble building below the temple is one of the more outstanding sights of the sanctuary. The statue of Kleobis was found on 10 May. Later the statue of Biton, his brother, was unearthed, and the giant pair dominate the museum of Delphi. They date from the time of an earlier temple to Apollo, and were the gifts of the people of Argos. As Herodotus tells their story—they were renowned for their great strength and both won prizes at the games. The ancient sculptor, in the style of early Greek workmanship, shows them as splendidly strong, yet gentle figures.

The following story is related of them: when the Argives were celebrating a festival of Hera, it was necessary that their mother, a priestess of the temple, should be drawn to the temple in a chariot; but the oxen did not come from the field in time, the young men therefore being pressed for time, put themselves beneath the yoke, and drew the car in which their mother sat.

The two brothers pulled the chariot through cheering crowds, for a distance of forty-five stades, about three miles.

The mother herself, transported with joy both on account of the action and its renown, stood before the image of Hera and prayed that the goddess would grant to Cleobis and Biton, her own sons, who had so highly honoured her, the greatest blessing that man could receive. After this prayer, when they had sacrificed and partaken of the feast, the youths fell asleep in the temple itself, and never awoke more, but met with such a termination of life. Whereupon the Argives, in commemoration of their piety caused the statues to be made and dedicated at Delphi.[1]

In 450 B.C., when Herodotus recalled the story of Kleobis and Biton, it was already ancient history, and the unearthing of the statues from the ground where they had been hidden for so long, brought immediate life to what had previously been just an account by a long dead historian.

Later that year, on 13 July, another statue was found. It came from much nearer to our own time, but was still over sixteen hundred years old. This was the beautiful, but soft, feminine portrayal of Antinous, the boy favourite of the Emperor Hadrian. Antinous died in Egypt and Hadrian ordered his statue to be displayed at Delphi.

By the end of 1893 the whole area round the temple bastion was cleared, and in the following year the excavations were extended. The treasury of the Syphnians at the outer edge of the Sacred Way, not far from the modern road, was reached during April and May. More and more pedestals and bases of monuments were found and during the first two years of excavation, E. Bourgnet, the most famous expert of the time on ancient inscriptions, often copied a hundred dedications and other writings a day.

In 1895 the working went deeper and the whole site was a

[1] Herodotus. *History*: I. 31.

scene of tremendous activity. On 28 April, the spring rains washed away some earth below the theatre, which lies on the hillside above the temple. The lower part of a bronze statue with a long skirt appeared, and it was with great excitement that the earth was carefully removed. A stone base with an inscription was found, together with two hind legs of a horse, and some fragments of hooves and a tail. On 1 May, higher up close to the theatre, the upper part of the statue, the Charioteer, was found, together with the right arm. In spite of a long search, the missing arm was never discovered. Homolle described it as appearing: 'In all the flower of its green-blue patina, without corrosion, or deformity or fault.' The preservation is certainly extraordinary. There was slight discolouration from a near-by sewer, but otherwise the bronze is undamaged, and when it was reassembled, the statue of the Charioteer was heralded as one of the most perfectly preserved bronze statues remaining from the times of Ancient Greece.

Each year the excavations were extended. The stadium was cleared in 1896. Apart from its outer wall, which had collapsed and fallen down the mountainside, it was found to be one of the finest in Greece. It had been restored by Herodes Atticus, an extremely rich Athenian, during Roman times. Herodes Atticus was a benefactor who rebuilt many of the public buildings of Greece, including the odeon and stadium in Athens, but nowhere is his work better preserved than in Delphi.

In 1898 they removed the old monastery, which had been associated with the Convent of Jerusalem on the other side of Parnassos, and excavated the gymnasium beneath it. The beautiful Tholos and the near-by temple of Athene Pronaia were reached in 1901.

In 1902 a small museum was erected near the sanctuary, to house the treasures that had been found. The museum was rebuilt by a German architect in 1938, and is now one of the richest of its kind in Greece. Everything that was found on the site was deposited there. Unlike many other archaeological sites, Delphi, which had been pillaged so much in the past, never suffered from the depredation of collectors in modern times, and as a result the museum gives a complete record of all that remains of Delphi.

The ten years between 1892 and 1902 were a time of massive engineering works. The removal of the old village, and the revelation of the ruins of the sanctuary which lay deep beneath it, occupied all the powers of the archaeologists, but the task of restoring Delphi to some semblance of its original form, and of deciphering a part of the mystery associated with the worship there, had only just begun. Over the years the stones of buildings had been scattered, many of them far from their original sites, and the first problem was one of regrouping them, as far as possible, in their original places. In some cases it was possible to re-erect the least damaged parts. Where stones were easily identified this replacement was possible because of the methods of Greek builders. In all the finest work of Greek masons, nothing was interchangeable, and every stone had its carefully planned place and fitted nowhere else. This skilful reconstruction was done in a few places to make it possible to envisage the general scale of the sanctuary, but, of even more importance to the archaeologists, it protected the remains from new damage, and enabled them to investigate underlying structures. In the best archaeological tradition there was no artificial placing of the stones for the benefit of tourists, or serious attempts at reconstruction, which, in a site of the size of Delphi, would in any case have been impossible.

The grandeur of the sanctuary is revealed with dramatic intensity from the ruins that remain, and the pillars that have been raised. The vast area of fallen walls and piled masonry that surrounds the temple on every side, confusing and incoherent though it appears to the visitor, has in fact been studied stone by stone by archaeologists.

The first reconstruction work that was undertaken in the sanctuary was the rebuilding of the Athenian treasury by J. Replat, between 1903 and 1906. This was made possible by money donated by a group of financiers of the city of Athens. In 1920 the isle of Chios gave similar help for the partial restoration of the great altar which stands in front of the temple. This altar was once presented to Delphi by the people of the same island. A special fund provided by the French government in 1938 made it possible to re-erect three columns and part of the entablature of the Tholos, the circular building built at the end of the fifth century and described as one of the most beautiful in Greece. The same fund provided for the raising of the eight columns of the temple of Apollo, one whole, the others in pieces, a work which was completed in 1941. In addition to major works of this kind, continued strengthening and preservation of existing structures takes place each year; a necessary precaution in the exposed situation of Delphi. Both Greek and French archaeologists continue the work of investigation and research, and at present the ancient fountain of Kassotis, high above the temple, and its associated buildings are being examined.

The ten years between 1892 and 1902 were called 'the Great Excavation' and it was once thought that most of the work was completed, but in many places the investigation had not gone further than Roman or Classical Greek times. Even though the statues and monuments no longer exist, Pausanias would recognize the sanctuary and the sacred path winding through the remains of the same buildings that he admired nearly 2,000 years ago, but beneath those buildings lie other structures dating from a far earlier age. New developments in scientific archaeology make it necessary to re-examine the discoveries made at the end of the nineteenth century, when excavation of the Classical Greek Age was of greatest interest to archaeologists.

There have been seventy-five years of almost continual research since the first official excavations started, and the range has extended to the very earliest days of pre-history, before the worship of Apollo came to Delphi, and far beyond the sanctuary itself to the whole area of Delphic territory. Confirmation of the stories and legends of Delphi have been found everywhere. At the lowest levels, below the present sanctuary, before the first temple was built between the years 1000 and 700 B.C., there are no signs of religious worship, and the site was apparently unoccupied, but when research was extended to the area beneath the temple of Athene Pronaia, objects belonging to the worship of Earth, the Mother-Goddess, were found.

It is obviously no coincidence that the only temple of a female deity in the sanctuary, in this case Athene, should be on the site of the earliest worship of the female goddess Ge.

It was here that the legendary conquest by Apollo of an older worship was confirmed, and given historical authenticity.

Between 1935 and 1939 research was extended to the remains of the old cities of Kirra and Krissos. The port of Kirra was found to be very ancient indeed, and may have been built by the Minoans from Crete, some time between 2,000 and 1,700 B.C., when the Minoans were the greatest sea-power in that part of the Mediterranean. Now it no longer exists, and the new town of Itea lies on the other side of the river mouth. Krissos, however, still remains on its original site. It is only a village now, but it has been inhabited through all the vicissitudes of wars and destruction for about 3,600 years. No other place in that part of Greece can show such continuity from Mycenean times to the present day. Because of its continual occupation, the prehistoric evidence is scattered. The only ancient pottery is broken and lies where it was discarded by its users, but more than sixty thousand of these broken sherds have been examined, and it has been possible to reconstruct eighty-eight pots.

From these finds J. Jannoray and H. van Effenterre have been able to present a picture of the probable course of events, in those years before recorded history. After the establishment of Kirra, it became obvious that it was in a dangerous position and very vulnerable to the raiders from the sea; it was, therefore, necessary to build a citadel inland. The high ground on which Krissos was built was easy to defend, and it had the added advantage that it commanded one of the few routes through the almost inaccessible mountains to the interior of the country. In course of time Krissos became the most important city of the region. Jannoray writes: 'At the upper valley of the Pleistos this town was well placed to be in some way, the junction point where there was a fusion of Cretan (Cycladic) influence coming from the sea and the continental tradition coming from over the land.'[1]

Although Krissos has become an unimportant village today, the arm of the sea, including the bay of Itea, which can be seen shining in the distance from the village of Delphi, is known as the Gulf of Krissos, and records the time when this country was known as 'the land of Krissos'. Delphi was then

[1] J. Jannoray and H. van Effenterre. Excavations at Kirra and Krissos. *Bulletin Hellénique*, LXII, 1938.

nothing but a small, sacred shrine, but with the coming of the Dorian Greek invaders and the establishment of the worship of Apollo, it increased its influence, until at last, many years afterwards, the whole region became part of the sacred Delphic domains.

The results of the excavations of Kirra and Krissos have only recently been published, and in due course they will be included in the volumes of the official records of excavations at Delphi, the *Fouilles de Delphes*. From the beginning of the undertaking there was a clear direction to the archaeologists that their work must be published or recorded in complete detail for the benefit of the scientific world in general, and this has been conscientiously done. There are now twenty-five volumes of the *Fouilles*, and Georges Daux, the present Director of the French School in Athens, who has been connected with the Delphic excavations for thirty-five years, looks forward confidently towards, at least, another twenty-five volumes before the work nears completion.

The first account of the main excavations of the temple and the sanctuary was in Volume II, edited by M. F. Courby. He wrote in his introduction:

When I accepted the starting of the architectural study of the Delphic sanctuary, perhaps I had not sufficiently realised the weight of the honour offered to me. Perhaps I was wrong to start, but I was unable to resist the very powerful attraction which these prodigious ruins exercised on me. If I had seen in advance all the effort which was to hinder the task, and the poor satisfaction the results were to give me, I think I would have left to others the task of assessing our work. For in this region of the sanctuary more than anywhere else perhaps, the difficulties are extreme and of all kinds. I do not refer only to the material complications . . . these are the lot of all excavators, but here, although we pose our questions with a passionate desire to obtain the answers, we are given no reply. Here in the most sanctified of all places, where life has been troubled by the deeds of men and nature, all that we have left are dumb ruins. I must leave it to others with better knowledge to solve the problems, only adding my own ideas when possible.

M. Courby was modest about his own contributions to our knowledge of Delphi but the central problem of the nature of the oracle and its working is still a subject for dispute and speculation, and perhaps it always will be, as long as we look for rational explanations for a mystical experience.

The American archaeologist, Leicester Holland, took up M. Courby's challenge, and produced his own theories which have not found much favour with the French, but in a matter that is so speculative cannot be ignored. Courby has described the discovery of the *adyton* within the temple: 'Within the temple, quite at one side, stood a little structure, the Adyton, sanctuary of the Oracle, and very old in origin. This small building was of two stories, the upper room for the consultants of the Oracle being built above an obscure crypt where, in the rocky floor, was supposed to be the mysterious fissure.'[1]

In the part of the temple foundation where the *adyton* was discovered, they found a block of limestone which was evidently part of a pavement. A channel cut in the top surface divides it roughly into two parts; on one part stood something nearly square in plan, and on the other a partly circular object. There are a number of holes in the block, some of which Courby suggested were made to lift the block into place, and the others, he said, were dowel holes for holding a circular monument. Leicester Holland wrote: 'This was obviously for the three legs and central columnar support of a metal tripod. The arrangement is not at all uncommon in Greek remains, and I am at a loss to see why, with his fertile imagination and clear insight, M. Courby has not suggested it here.'[2] The same block is shown to tourists every day, by the guides of Delphi, as the site of the original oracular tripod, as was suggested by Professor Holland, but the explanation has not been wholly accepted by the French archaeologists.

Professor Holland expanded his theories about the working of the oracle. The tripod stood on one side of this block and the *omphalos* on the circular base next to it, and branches of laurel were placed in the small holes on each side of the tripod base. The hole in the centre of the *omphalos* communicated by a tube to a cave beneath the *adyton*. The Pythia went into this cave 'ostensibly to get the water of Kassotis. She actually lit a

[1] M. F. Courby. *Fouilles de Delphes*. Tome II, 1927.
[2] Leicester Holland. Mantic Mechanism at Delphi. *American Journal of Archaeology*, XXXVII, 1933.

brazier there, and then coming up again, and mounting on the tripod, inhaled fumes piped through the floor beneath her feet.' The bystanders seeing the fumes arising mysteriously from the *omphalos*, and from the cave below, would be convinced of the reality of a secret emanation. Although it is possible that this stone was once the site of the famous oracular tripod, the explanation of the making of the vapour is hardly credible. The Greeks were not innocent of using mechanical tricks of this kind to impress ignorant worshippers, but the account given by Plutarch do not suggest that this was the case in Delphi. The mystery of the oracle remains, as perhaps it always will.

The early excavators were often disappointed, unreasonably so, it seems to us now, after so much wealth of discovery. Even the great Homolle in 1894, wrote: 'The temple on which so much hope had rested, has been a great deception. Of the edifice built in the 4th century, we have not recovered a single metope or fragment of a frieze, not even a little finger of a figure which had come from the pediment.' It has never been an easy task, but the work of long and devoted scholarship has certainly justified itself time and again. The major excavations are completed, but fresh discoveries continue to be made. Examination of the ruins reveals still more of the life of the ancient builders of Delphi. A clear picture of the actions of the men who worked in the sanctuary can even be reconstructed from the stonework itself. One of the more remarkable examples of this deductive analysis was given by M. Bousquet in his excavation of the treasury of Kyrene in 1937.

After the destruction of the temple in 373 B.C., the Kyrenians decided to build a treasury in the sanctuary. Because of the dangers from landslides and waterfalls, they chose a site well away from the other monuments at the edge of the sanctuary wall, over to the right side. A visitor to the sanctuary walking up from the entrance to the Sacred Way, and looking up at the temple above, would see in front of him to one side the front of the treasury bathed in sunlight, from dawn to early afternoon. A separate stairway led to it from the Sacred Way. This treasury was built partly from inferior Pentelic marble and partly from the highly prized marble from Paros, and in his account Bousquet wrote:

M

Perhaps when he went to the marble suppliers, the architect found that they had in stock two different kinds of marble. The reason being that, during the sacred war, a number of the shaped blocks had mysteriously disappeared. A more likely explanation is that it was decided to enlarge the original plan for the treasury project, which obliged the architect of 330 B.C. to buy a supplementary supply. This was difficult in Delphi, as the price had gone up since the war— the stocks of Paros marble were difficult to obtain and were very dear, and so reserved mostly for sculpture. It is known that the situation of Delphi, 500 metres above the sea, and the difficulty of the road from Khirra, had a serious influence on the price of building materials.

The architect completed his building with a small quantity of Pentelic marble he had come across, which was not all of good quality. It must be realised, that, however much we appreciate Pentelic marble today, it was not thought so highly of in ancient times. It was a conveniently placed material for the construction of the Parthenon in Athens, when the cost of Parian marble was so high, but no doubt a great sculptor like Phidias realised that only Paros marble was really good for sculpture. Pentelic marble was of course sent to Delphi from Attica, because in Athens it was the local marble, and Athenian builders might like to have used their own local stone. Perhaps the builders of the Kyrenian Treasury bought the surplus marble from another building, which had recently been completed. Blue and red paint disguised the difference between the two marbles, and so justified the economic subterfuge of the master craftsman.[1]

Bousquet went a great deal further in analysing the motives of the builders of the Kyrenian treasury, although his evidence has been disputed. As we know, the sanctuary of Delphi was so important to the Greeks that they dedicated there the finest of their achievements. The greatest artists and craftsmen submitted the very best of their work as an offering to Apollo, and as a dedication from the nation which sent them to Delphi. Bousquet observed that the treasury of Kyrene was plain and simply built, but he also knew that there was a strong school of the Pythagoreans in Kyrene. 'To them, Apollo was the god of the mathematicians and in the treasury of Kyrene they expressed in marble the most complex mathematical relations as a gift of their skill to the god,' he wrote.

His conclusions were based on the measurement of the stones of the treasury, and in particular by the dimensions of

[1] Jean Bousquet. *Fouilles de Delphes*. Treasury of Kyrene, 1952.

a block which formed the door post of the inner room of the building. He observed what appeared to be the use of many mathematical formulae including square and cube roots and the ratio of π to $\frac{1}{\pi}$.

Bousquet's theory about the treasury of the Kyrenians was quite a conceivable one. It was known that Apollo was said to have encouraged the use of mathematics, and Plutarch once told a story to illustrate this. An oracle ordered the people of Delos to double the size of their great altar, but they found that the solution was not as easy as they thought. 'The oracle was given commanding the doubling of the cubical dimensions of the altar, not the linear, which latter any mason could have done by simple measurement. It is a problem requiring the utmost skill in geometry.' The Delians, therefore, sent messengers to Plato to obtain his advice. Plato's reply was that the god did not ask for an exact solution, which in fact is impossible, but was giving them a command to turn from political squabbling to the peaceful study of geometry and philosophy. Plutarch added: 'In the same way the god, by giving forth responses with double meanings, promotes and establishes logic, as being indispensable for all such as intend to understand him rightly.'[1]

Although archaeology as a science requires facts and proofs, and workers in the field do not approve of a fanciful speculation with insufficient evidence to support it, archaeology is also an art requiring imagination and an insight into the motives and thoughts of the men who lived in the distant past. From a small change in the quality of stone used, and from the dimensions of some of those stones, Bousquet deduced his picture of the craftsmen of 330 B.C., and showed a human and understanding approach to them.

More than any other archaeological site in Greece, Delphi was disappointing in its supply of concrete facts, as Courby discovered, but no other site has such a power to stir the imagination of anyone sensitive to its influence. Gerhart Hauptmann, the German dramatist wrote:

One thinks of Apollo, one thinks of Dionysos, but in these surroundings it is not of their images in stone or bronze that one thinks,

[1] Plutarch. *Moralia.*

rather one thinks of the true idol, the primitive image of wood, of which no trace has come down to us. Here and there one beholds gods, luminous, immaterial, visionary; chiefly, however, one recognises them in their actions. Here the Gods are invisibly present; and so, also like them, do the daimons people nature invisibly.

Is the chthonic spring really dried up? Have the daimons really left the Oracle? Are most of them dead, as they say the great Pan is dead? And is the great Pan really dead? I believe that every other spring of pre-Christian life is dried up rather than the Pythian . . . and here to me among these sun-cracked ruins is the whole mystery and the daimons and the Gods and Pan who they said was dead . . . are all present.[1]

Plutarch once said, 'Although Earth sends up numerous streams, those which rise at Delphi alone have power to fill the soul with ecstacy, and inspire men to conceive visions.' Hauptmann added, 'Now we esteem this inspiration but little, and generally speaking, do not wish to make that profound dedication with which sacred intoxication is linked,' but new efforts to restore the 'Delphic Idea' were to be made. This time it was by poets and musicians, for Apollo was the god of poetry and music, as well as of science and reason. The archaeological awakening of the site of Delphi, and the revelalation of its ancient sanctuary, was followed by another attempt to revive something of its original spiritual force.

[1] Gerhart Hauptmann. *Griechischer Frühling. A Record of Travel in Greece*, 1908.

WHEN the archaeologists moved the old village of Kastri, and pulled down the houses and churches, one part remained undisturbed. This was the chapel and little burial ground which still rests peacefully among the cypress trees, high up on the hillside, above the ruined sanctuary of Apollo. It is quiet there except for the murmur of the wind and the low sound of the mule bells from the old village threshing floor where the pack animals are tethered. Tourists seldom visit the burial ground. The old women in their black dresses and headcloths move occasionally among the graves, sometimes relighting an icon lamp before a faded photograph of the dead, and the olive oil from the simple lamp, a wick floating in a bowl of oil, drips in libation on to the ancient, disturbed earth. Some of the simple graves are new, but others, amid the debris of distant funeral rites, are very old and have been re-opened. It was always the custom to move the dead after a number of years, making room for new burials, a custom that we know is at least 3,500 years old, but in the corner of the burial ground, next to the ancient wall, there are more permanent graves and memorial stones, with inscriptions in English. Among them is the grave of the American poet, George Cram Cook. His name is forgotten now by a new generation, but in 1924 when he died, the poets of Greece met together and made an appeal to their government. The Greek government agreed to their request and presented a stone from the temple of Apollo, to be used as a headstone for his grave; an honour which is unique in modern Greece, where archaeological remains are, quite rightly, preserved with the greatest care.

George Cram Cook was born in Iowa in 1873, the son of a good American family. He went from the State University to Harvard, and there he soon developed an intense love of the Classical Greek language and, as has happened to many young poets, this became a romantic yearning for Greece itself. When he was twenty, he had an opportunity to visit Greece with a friend who was going there to study archaeology, and he wrote to his father: 'All this year Greek has been unfolding its beauty. The country is becoming for me, as for many others, as a lost fatherland. . . . I sit and dream of Greece. I hear, see, the blue waves of the Aegean beating on the shore.'[1]

There was no money then for him to make the journey, and he did not go to Greece until many years later, but his early love had a profound influence on the course of his life. His second wife, Susan Glaspell, wrote after his death: 'He grieved because the world has now forgotten the beautiful vitality of that dead nation. There grew upon him a sense of mystery and futility in the lives of men and nations.'

Like many young intellectuals at the end of the nineteenth century, Cook was caught up in enthusiasm for the coming of a new age of humanism. He shocked his friends and relations in conservative Iowa, by announcing that he was an anarchist, but they concluded that he was harmless enough. There was a great deal of talk by young idealists, about free-love, the emancipation of women, and the coming of a new society, but the forces of industrial and materialist progress went on unchecked.

Cook's socialism was always linked with his dream of a new cultural revolution; he wrote, 'Unless the Socialist movement is going to make room in itself for a culture as broad and imaginative as any aristocratic culture, it would be better for the world that it perish from the earth.'

Always too, he looked back to a world of Ancient Greece, when the aspirations of men so nearly produced an ideal society and yet failed. In his imagination: 'There spread before him, as between receding clouds, the Ancient Hellas. Her temples gleamed unruined upon the hills; her smokeless cities shone upon the shores of land locked bays, her sunny slopes were rich with olive-grove and vineyard; her quick eyed unhastening citizens acted for him the comedies of their long past lives.'

In 1913 George Cram Cook married Susan Glaspell and between them they started the Little Theatre movement, which they hoped would bring new life and excitement to the stage. For a number of years this theatre fulfilled all their hopes, and

[1] Susan Glaspell. *The Road to the Temple*, 1928.

gave an outlet for the presentation of unfashionable, outspoken plays, until at last it began to become a commercial success, and its original inspiration faded. Rather than let the theatre, 'whose motives were spiritual', become a voice of mediocrity in a commercial world, they closed it down, and Cook exclaimed, 'It is time to go to Greece.' On 1 March 1922, he sailed from New York, never to return.

In 1922 Greece was an unhappy country. The grinding poverty had been intensified by the flood of refugees coming from Turkey, who had solved her minority problems by ruthlessly ejecting all Greeks on her territory. In the mountains, bandits still preyed on the shepherds and villagers, and feuds and bloodshed were often part of their daily lives. In spite of the disturbed and sometimes violent world of Greece, to George Cram Cook it was a homecoming. In the beauty and immense vitality of that land, he found no disillusionment and no betrayal of the dreams of his youthful days. With his family he went to live in Delphi, where he was loved and accepted by the village people as one of themselves, and here again he found: 'The wonder of the world is so much vaster than anyone else seems to have felt.'

In summer-time they went up with the shepherds on to the meadows of Parnassos, returning in winter to their home in Delphi. Cook astonished the simple countrymen with his love of animal life, especially birds, those little birds of Parnassos which fed from his hand. Before he came, the shepherds thought of birds as a prey to be hunted and eaten. During the warm summer evenings, on the mountain or by the winter fires, Cook talked to the villagers about Delphi and its wonderful history. He told them, too, that there had always been voices there, and that the people of Delphi were the inheritors of a spiritual power that could conquer the world.

Day after day, the tall bearded figure, dressed in a homespun shepherd's cloak, walked among the ruins of the ancient city, thinking of its past and dreaming of the future. Cook planned to write a play about Delphi, in which all the village would participate. It was to be a dramatic synthesis of past and present, in which the philosophers of the ancient world talked with the philosophers of today in a newly awakened sanctuary of Delphi. 'It could be another Oberammergau, and straight from the people! Too long that old theatre has waited for the people of Delphi to return!' he said.

In the winter of 1924 Delphi was snowed up and Cook fell ill. It was Christmas and the village was full of gaiety and excitement. Friends called in sympathy for the sudden attack of what was thought to be influenza, and hoped he would soon be back to sing and drink with them, in the company he loved so much. They told him a strange story. One of the small birds had not migrated with the others, but had stayed behind to be near him. It lived in the warmth of the kitchen, feeding happily on the scraps of food it found there.

Each day Cook grew more ill. With great difficulty an American doctor got through the drifts to see him, but by then he was too sick to be moved to hospital. A few days later, at the age of 51, George Cram Cook died from an infection he may have caught from a pet dog, one of the animals he had cherished so lovingly.

When he was a young man he had written the lines which Susan Glaspell quoted in his biography,[1]

> The leaves have their life although unlike mine own,
> And life is fading from them for all time.
> I would, fair leaves, whose fading is so fair,
> That you could know your beauty gives me joy
> For I would know my own death beautiful
> To some eternal watcher of the world.

George Cram Cook left very little behind, some poetry and a few plays; his morality play about Delphi remained unfinished, but to the people of Delphi he became a legend. He was a visitor from a foreign land, who had talked strangely about birds and said: 'They are very small, and they are not like us, but maybe they are more wonderful than we are,' but he was also the man who had inspired them with a realization of how important their village had been and might still be.

In the midst of their Christmas festival, the whole village was suddenly stricken with grief, and all the celebrations stopped. A few days later they carried him up to the little graveyard and there buried him. On the marble slab over his grave is carved the epitaph he had written himself.

[1] Susan Glaspell. *The Road to the Temple.*

The Thyiades. The origin of
this Pentelic marble acanthus-
leaved column found at Delphi
is not known, but the lovely
dancing girls are thought to
represent Thyiads.

The Apollo by Phidias
from the temple of Zeus
at Olympia. He
signified the profound
principle of man's
aspirations towards
light and reason, away
from the dark forces of
materialism.
Photo: V. & N. Tombazi

A scene which was a
popular subject for
many vase paintings
showed Apollo's dispute
with Herakles, who
attempted to steal the
tripod. *British Museum*

East frieze of the Siphnian treasury. Battle of Greeks and Trojans.
Photo: V. & N. Tombazi

Herakles—a metope
from the north side of
the treasury of the
Athenians.

North frieze of the Siphnian treasury. Battle of the gods and giants.
Photo: V. & N. Tombazi

Being now well affured, that *Salona* was not *Delphos*, but the *Amphiffa* of old ; we enquired of our Hoft, whether there were no antient Ruins of a Town in our way between this and *Livadia* ? He told us, That there were many at *Caftri*, a Village about mid-way: So we fpake with feveral Janizaries to conduct us thither, and thence to *Livadia* and *Thebes*. Put not agreeing upon the Price, we took the Brother of *Mahomet Bafha*, and parted very early next Morning. For Monfieur *Spon*'s going into the Water at the Fountain, above the Town, had made fome of the *Turks* to murmur, and to fufpect us to be Spies.

A little way from the Town we foorded a Brook, which joyns with the other Stream in the Plain ; but are both near loft in watering them, before they come to the Sea.   After a Mile or two Riding, we looked about, and faw another *Janizary* following us, of thofe we had fpoken to over night : which we were refolved to keep alfo ; thinking, until we were better acquainted with the Country, we could not be too fecure.   So we were now eight ftrong ; *viz.* our two Janizaries, our *Greek*, our three *Hagoiatics*, or Guides, who were the owners of our Horfes, Monfieur *Spon*, and my felf.   We foon began to mount the Ridges of the Mountain *Parnaffus*, by a very bad rough way, South-Eaftwards, until we arrived, in four or five Hours time, at *Caftri* ; which we no fooner approached, but we concluded, that it was undoubtedly the Remainder of the famous City of *Delphos*. CASTRI. DELPHOS.

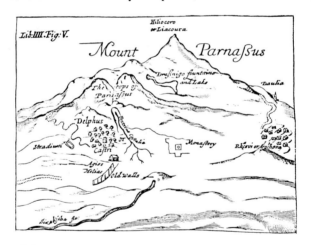

Lib:IIII.Fig:V.

Hilio coro or Liacoura.

Mount   Parnaſsus

Caftri, or *Delphos*, is fituate on the South-fide of the Mountain *Parnaffus*, fomething inclining to the Weft ; not on the top, nor at the foot of the Mountain: for it hath a great way to the Plains of *Criffa* below it, and much more to the Mountains above it.   The high Cliffs in fight above it from the Town, feem to end in two points ; whence I judged it was call'd of old, *Biceps Parnaffus :* For it hath many more tops,

S f   and

and much higher than thefe, being a very great Mountain: But thefe two tops feen from *Delphos*, hide all the reft. Between which the Water falls, in great abundance, after Rain or Snow, and hath worn them almoft afunder. There is alfo a Fountain, with a very plentiful Source of Water, continually iffuing out from among thofe Rocks, juft under that Separation: which by the Marble Steps defcending to it, and the Niches made in the Rock for Statues above it, fhould be the Fountain *Caftalia*, that fo infpired the antient Poets. Its Stream falleth down Southward a very deep, and narrow Precipice; where it foon joyneth with the River *Pleiftos*, feparating Mount *Cirphis* from *Parnaffus*: whence it runs by *Criffa* Southwards, and falleth into the Bay of *Salona*. Weft, and Northweft likewife, *Delphos* hath a Defcent; but not fo fteep: Northwards it is backed with the double-headed Cleft of *Parnaffus*. But, that no Doubt might remain, but this was *Delphus*, we found feveral Infcriptions bearing that Name in antient *Greek* Characters: of which this Fragment, I brought with me, and is now at *Oxford*, is one.

IA.

```
.ΤΥΧΑ ΔΕΛΦΟ...
.. ΑΝΓΙΑΤΡΩΝΑ...
.. ΩΝΙΟ ΕΥΔΩΡΩΝ..
.. ΑΡΚΟΥ ΒΟΙΩΤΟΙΣ..
ΤΑΝΑΓΡΑΣ ΑΥΤΟΙΣ
Ι ΕΝΓΟΝΟΙΣ ΠΡΟΞΕ
Ν ΠΡΟΜΑΝΤΕΙΑΝ
.ΕΛΙΑΔΑΣ ΥΛΙΑΝ
ΠΡΟΕΔΡΙΑΝ ΠΡΟΔΙΚΙ
ΑΝ ΕΠΙ ΤΙΜΑΝ ΚΑΘΑΠΕΡ
.ΔΕΛΦΟΙΣ ΑΡΧΟΝΤΟΣ
ΘΟΙΝΙΩΝΟΣ ΒΟΛΕΥ
.ΝΤΩΝ. ΣΩΠΟΔΟΡΟΥ
```

I need not tell you what this Place was in antient times: All the World knows, how famous *Delphos* hath been for the Oracle of *Apollo* there, confulted for fo many Ages together. But its antient Glory is now vanifhed; and it remains Great, at prefent, only in the Writings of the Antients. Before we entred within the Compafs of the (former) City, we obferved feveral Grottoes cut in the Rocks, with feveral Partitions, as we conceived, to bury the Dead; as believing, that the antient Sanctity, and Refpect had to this Place, would not permit to bury the Dead within the Walls; no more than at *Delos*, the other famous Oracle of *Apollo*. Mounting a little higher, by a way cut out of the Rocks, we entred through a Paffage, where we thought the antient Gates might have been: from whence we faw the Town of *Caftri* hard by; and defcending thence a little further, we went into a Church on the right hand, called St *Helias*; where we found the laft, and fome other pieces of white Marble, with Infcriptions on them. At the Door of this Church is another great Stone, with fome Lines of an Infcription, which we copied as well as we could, and where I thought, that I read the Name of *Delphos* again. This feems to be the Place moft likely for the Temple of *Apollo* to have been fituated in; although now no

Remains

Above and opposite   The account of the rediscovery of Delphi after a thousand years was given by Wheeler in *Journeys,* published in 1682. *British Museum*

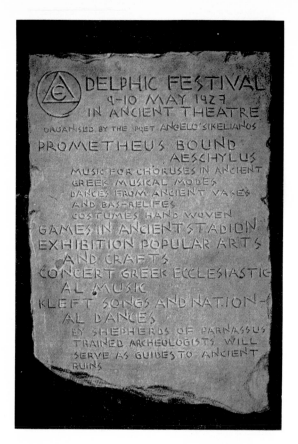

This announcement of the Delphic Festival was sent all over the world by Eva Sikelianos.

Prometheus Bound, Delphic Festival 1927. Mme Kakouri played Io, the cow pursued by Zeus, in the remarkable mask used at that performance.

M. Bourlos as Prometheus, in the costume woven and designed by Eva Sikelianos.

All photographs on these two pages by courtesy of Mme Katerina Kakouri

Mme Pratzika, chorus-leader, standing with M. Bourlos.

Eva Sikelianos, centre, with long red hair, next to Io (Mme Kakouri).

The Korykian cave. Difficult of access and invisible from below, the cave is very dark and deep. Anastasias Karagicas, who accompanied the author, is one of the shepherds of Parnassos. Times change and the traditional fustanella is now seldom worn, but the simple dignity and hospitality of shepherds like Anastasias is as real today as it ever was.

Above Delphi stands the monument to Anghelos Sikelianos, in the place where he had dreams of reviving its vanished grandeur and of making it once more a source of inspiration to people.

> I hear the mountain stream.
> Pouring in beauty that rhythmic water
> Does not need to be more than itself.
> But I
> Spirit
> Have no reason for living
> Unless somehow for spirit somewhere
> Life is immortal.

Beneath the name on the stone, the sculptor carved the outline of the little bird that Cook loved so much, and which became so tame when he fed it during those summers on Parnassos.

Another stone was taken from the temple of Apollo and erected at the head of the grave, and at the request of the Greek poets it was carved with the verse which Cook wrote in Delphi. The lines commemorated the Greece which he saw as an experiment of man's spirit; an experiment which failed, and yet could be everlastingly renewed.

> Not in the Parthenon
> The temple of the shape of the mind
> Thrust upward from the Attic promontory
> In proud affirmation
> To be for ever
> The image of Intellectual beauty.
> Knowing its worth
> More deeply here
> In the heart that is us all
> The instinct of the hollow of the hills
> Not knowing its own aim
> Built blindly for the Greece
> Which could not be.

The poets of modern Greece honoured George Cram Cook and it is in them that the fire and spirit of the Ancient Greek world has renewed itself most vividly. One of them in particular tried passionately to revive the Delphic spirit in the modern world. This was Anghelos Sikelianos, the poet whose dreams not only gave a new vigour to the artistic life of modern Greece, but have inspired men ever since to think of a revival of the 'Delphic Idea'.

When George Cram Cook went to Delphi, the people of

Greece, in spite of their poverty, had retained the vitality and reverence for life which their ancestors had felt. There was also a continuous tradition among the shepherds and country people, a tradition of singing and dancing, which had remained with them and linked them with the distant past. Sikelianos saw, in the traditional memories of these country people, an unconscious feeling for an earlier knowledge, which was now lost. To him the world of the senses, and the intense love of life these humble people showed, was a direct consequence of the supernatural forces which were once realized in the worship of Apollo at Delphi. In his poetry he sought to rediscover the ancient, supernatural realities without which man's relationship with the universe was incomplete.

While Sikelianos was visiting America, he was introduced one day to Eva Palmer, a girl with long red hair and a deep voice, and very soon found that she shared his love of Greece, and his dream of reviving once more the lost glory of Delphi. They fell in love and were married.

Eva Palmer was the daughter of an American millionaire; she was educated at Bryn Mawr and the Sorbonne. She was interested in the Greek Theatre, but no one then realized that she was going to play such a fiery role in its revival. She met the Duncans, Isadora and her brother Raymond, who had both fallen so much under the spell of Ancient Greece, that they often dressed eccentrically in Classical Greek clothes. Isadora Duncan, the dancer, had many years earlier, with not much success, taken a choir of Greek boys round Europe in an attempt to revive what she interpreted as ancient Greek choral singing and dancing. Unfortunately the Greek boys terrorized the staff of hotels, throwing beefsteaks at the heads of waiters, and even crept out at night to meet low company, of which Isadora Duncan disapproved. In spite of their setbacks, the Duncans inspired Eva Palmer with a burning desire to revive Greek Theatre, and when she met Anghelos Sikelianos, it seemed that providence had a hand in their meeting.

After their marriage the couple went to live in Greece, where Eva learnt to speak fluent Greek and threw herself fervently into the plans for the revival of Delphi.

Delphi was the spiritual centre of the whole ancient world, and Sikelianos had dreams of reviving its vanished grandeur, of making it once more a source of inspiration to all people. He wanted to gather artists of all kinds at Delphi, so that the spirit of Apollo would fall on them, and, under the influence of the old gods, they would form an 'intellectual *élite* who would rule the world'. After all, it was Apollo who had announced the new law that the earth should belong to poets and musicians.

Eva was more practical and threw herself, with intense fervour, into making the dream of a revival of the Delphic festival a reality. It was decided to bring back ancient Classical drama to the theatre in Delphi for the first time for 2,000 years, and a production of *Prometheus Bound* was planned.

Anghelos Sikelianos had gathered round him a group of dedicated young Greeks, who entered into the scheme with tremendous enthusiasm, helping in the practical work of producing the drama, filled with the conviction that they belonged to a Delphic brotherhood of great spiritual significance. The people of Delphi, having been prepared for a festival of this kind by George Cram Cook, a few years earlier, joined whole-heartedly in the preparations.

Eva Sikelianos was determined that the festival should be as perfect as possible, and that every detail should be attended to with infinite care. She studied the designs on the pottery of Ancient Greece, not only to discover the kind of clothes that were worn then, but also how each fold of a garment fell; on her own loom she wove materials that would match as nearly as possible the cloths of two thousand years earlier. The costumes were made with such care that at least one of them has been preserved in a museum, as an example of classical Greek dress. She poured the money of her inheritance into the scheme; everthing had to be done correctly, regardless of expense. If gold ornaments were called for, then they had to be of real gold.

Eva Sikelianos came like a whirlwind, designing and directing, organizing and inspiring everyone with her energy. She followed the original theory that had interested Isadora Duncan, that in Byzantine church music lay clues to the ancient choruses of Classical Greek drama, but she brought a new insight into the singing and dancing of the chorus.

It was announced that the festival was to take place on 9 and 10 May 1927. The first day was reserved for the visiting *élite* and the second was for the local people and friends of the 'Delphic Brotherhood'. The notices which Eva Sikelianos sent out all over the world read:

DELPHIC FESTIVAL
9–10 May 1927
In Ancient Theatre
Organised by the poet Anghelos Sikelianos
Prometheus Bound, Aeschylus.
Music for choruses in ancient Greek musical modes
Dances from ancient vases and bas-reliefs
Costumes hand woven.
Games in ancient Stadion
Exhibition Popular Arts and Crafts.
Concert Greek Ecclesiastical Music
Kleft songs and national dances by shepherds of Parnassos.
Trained archaeologists will serve as guides to ancient ruins.

The festival games were dedicated to the memory of George Cram Cook, and in the stadium young Greek soldiers ran and wrestled in the carefully reproduced armour of the ancient hoplites, and danced the Pyrrhic dances.

The festival did not run smoothly. At the beginning of May 1927 all the preparations were completed, but no audience of world intellectuals arrived. The National Tourist Organization of Greece had advised them not to come. Delphi, at that time, was not equipped to house a large number of important visitors, there were no amenities or sufficient hotels available. It was not considered advisable to house them in tents, as the visitors to the festivals of ancient times had been accommodated. It was feared that the difficulties would discourage, permanently, the kind of tourists the National Tourist Organization had worked so hard to attract. Eva was in despair; she later wrote: 'My last hope was gone. We had no answers to our small advertisements. We had requested our own people not to attend the first performance as the second one was reserved for them. With everything ready, the theatre would have remained empty; we sent many telegrams to friends and others, inviting them all to come. So expenses for boats, cars, food and hotels had to be paid by us.'[1] Thus at the last minute an

[1] 1951. Letter to Mme Katerina Kakouri, who has kindly given me permission to quote from it.

audience gathered for the first theatrical performance in Delphi, after two thousand years.

Technically and artistically the performance of *Prometheus Bound* exceeded all expectations. No one had quite realized the effect Delphi itself would have on the play, or how the actors' voices would echo against the high walls of the Phaedriades. 'Two eagles swept down from the sky over Prometheus and many of the spectators wept.'

Eva Sikelianos had poured all her money into the Delphic revival and now it was all gone. Against the advice of Anghelos she returned to the United States, hoping to arouse interest in their plans, and to find financial support. Anghelos Sikelianos believed that it was not possible to convey the meaning of the Delphic purpose in 'a place which was absorbed in material values' and, as Eva wrote: 'He was right. The America I remembered did not exist any longer. . . . The atmosphere was suffocating. . . . The long journey which I made giving lectures barely covered its costs. I returned to Paris to study: the Delphic task seemed to have come to an end.'

Once again, in 1930, there was a festival, about which it was said: 'The directors of the Delphic Festival hope to gather kindred spirits from the world over, and here cement a brotherhood whose members will spread peace and good will afar.' This time the project was supported by the National Tourist Organization of Greece, but the old fire and enthusiasm had gone, and hopes of making a spectacular revival of the glory of Delphi died.

Eva Sikelianos returned once more to America, estranged from Anghelos. The war came, in which he courageously defied the enemy who occupied Greece, inspiring people with his brave words. Then in 1951 he died.

The survivors of the 'Delphic Brotherhood' who attended his funeral were desolated. One of them wrote to Eva to tell her of their common loss and begged her to return once more to Greece. She was by then an aged and dying woman, but she returned to Delphi, the scene of those triumphant days twenty-five years earlier. Her friends greeted her with honours, and among them she died. They placed a pomegranate in her hand and a coin between her lips and buried her in the old graveyard of Delphi, near the grave of George Cram Cook, who also dreamed of a new revival of the 'Delphic Idea'. At her funeral the village women of Delphi, who had once acted in the chorus under her direction, quite spontaneously started to sing the words of Aeschylus' *Prometheus*, which they had learnt for the festival in 1927: 'Fear nothing we are all your friends. We have flown to this mountain on racing wings. . . .'

The sad venture to restore Delphi to its ancient glory was ended at last, but the Americans, who had once been too busy with their commercial and material values, did not entirely forget Eva Sikelianos and her dreams. In 1957, to commemorate the revival of Delphi in 1927, a performance of Classical Greek drama was given in Athens by 'Greek and American stars from Broadway and Hollywood'. The United States Delphic committee was comprised of a galaxy of famous people, lovers of Greece and admirers of the aspirations of Sikelianos: Edith Hamilton, Judith Anderson, Maxwell Anderson, Clarence Derwent, Helen Hayes, Frederic March, H. E. George Melas, Elsa Maxwell, H. E. Christian Palamas, Spyros Skouros, Tennessee Williams and Ned Manerino.

The plans of the poet Sikelianos for the restoration of Delphi, as the centre of a new order, and the place from which the poets and musicians would rule the world, seemed at that time doomed to be a failure. In spite of the enthusiasm of his disciples for the romantic dreams of 1927, the festivals were discontinued. Attention to detail of dress and research into the ancient musical modes produced only a copy of an age long past, and no careful study could reproduce its exact form. To the spectators, the festivals were a dramatic and exciting pageant of an ancient world which had vanished for ever.

Although that attempt to revive the festival was not successful, the effort was not a wasted one. Over the years which followed it was to have a decisive effect on all aspects of intellectual life in Greece. The Greeks had only been liberated for a hundred years, and it appeared that they had lost all contact with their ancient past. In order to become a nation of equal stature to their European neighbours, in the theatre and arts, they had developed a culture which owed most of its impetus to other European influences. As Sikelianos had realized, there still existed, in folk traditions and religious rituals, an unlimited treasury of singing, dancing and speech, which had its roots in the distant past and its beginning in primeval religious worship. The 'Delphic Idea' which Anghelos and Eva Sikelianos tried to revive in 1927 brought this wealth of culture to the attention of Greek musicians and writers. It was no longer to be simply a process of studying ancient musical notation, or the designs on pottery, which at its best could only produce an imperfect imitation of the world of the past, but of accepting the spirit which motivated the men of Classical Greece, which is still very much alive. Greek music of today has a characteristic rhythm which is unsymmetrical and a unique, irregular beat which is full of the power to make people want to dance. Plutarch once said that the followers of Dionysos: 'Sing dithyrambic songs full of passion and of transformation that involves a certain wandering and scattering.'

It does not seem unreasonable to find evidence of the dithyramb alive today, and to use it once more in the chorus of the theatre, over which Dionysos once presided and where his spirit is still to be found, or to recognize it in the music and dancing, which is such a joyful part of the lives of Greek people, wherever they may be.

15 · The Delphic Idea

ANGHELOS SIKELIANOS saw in the pagan mysteries of Orphism a supernatural reality, and sought to restore something of those ancient beliefs to our modern world. He contemplated a spiritual revival of the 'Delphic Idea', as he called it, and one step towards this was the restoration of the Classical Greek drama to the theatre of Delphi. By one of the strange quirks of history, pagan traditions survived longer amongst actors than among any other body of people, and his efforts to revive the spirit of the ancient gods could not have been expressed in a better way than through the theatre. The Byzantine Christian Church was hostile to theatrical performances. John Chrysostom, who lived at the end of the fourth century A.D., wrote about the theatre at Antioch, 'Yea, and in that place there are foul words and fouler gestures, and the dressing of the hair has the same purpose, and the gait, and the costume and the voice, and the languishing movement of the limbs, and the rolling of the eyes, and the flutes and pipes, and the action, and the plots and everything, in short, is full of the utmost licentiousness.'[1]

In every age, including our own, there has been this kind of criticism of the theatre, at times with justification, but it was not because of the moral dangers that there was so much opposition by the Church. It was because, traditionally, performances in the theatre had been sacred to the gods and were once part of the rites of Dionysos. In A.D. 691, the Council in Trullo, in its Sixty-Second Canon, officially prohibited all comic, satyric or tragic masks, and it was clear that it referred expressly to the Ancient Greek theatre of Aristophanes and Euripides. In spite of the ban, the theatre flourished, with the result that mimic dancers or actors were excommunicated. They were refused the last sacrament and were excluded from baptism and holy communion. As they were also prevented, by law, from giving up their careers, they therefore had to remain

[1] Translated by E. Wellesz in *Byzantine Music and Hymnography*.

pagans. Eventually these harsh laws were rescinded, but through-out history the position of an actor has often been regarded as an equivocal one, in spite of the great appreciation for his art.

Today, when the portrayal of pagan gods on the stage is unlikely to offer a serious challenge to Christianity, there has been an enthusiastic revival of Classical Greek theatre, especially in Greece itself. There are festivals of these ancient dramas every year in Athens, Epidaurus, Dodona and other centres in Greece, and travelling companies have received tremendous acclaim in many other parts of the world. It was in 534 B.C. that the tragic actor, Thespis, won the prize at the first true drama contest in history, which had been inaugurated by Pisistratus, Tyrant of Athens, in honour of Dionysos. Thespis, for the first time, carried on a dialogue with the rest of the chorus, and in this way the Greek theatre was born. It was proposed by the International Theatre Institute that the anniversary of Thespis' achievement, 2,500 years ago, should be celebrated throughout the world.

Once again men's eyes turned towards Delphi, the one-time international meeting-place. To celebrate the Thespian anniversary, the Greek Government are making plans to establish a Delphic International Drama Festival, to be held every two years. In the words of the organizers, it is intended to 'revive the spirit of the ancient Amphictyons, the intellectual and artistic meeting-place of all those serving the high ideal of the Theatre, and particularly Ancient Drama'. Eminent theatrical companies from all parts of the world have been invited to take part in the festivals by presenting their own productions of classical drama. Each of the nations represented has a common interest in the theatre, but with widely diverging cultural backgrounds they will come to Delphi to share with others their own contribution to the art of the theatre. In return, Delphi, which is unlike any other stage setting, inevitably imposes its own exciting intensity on every play performed.

As a contribution to the re-awakening interest in Delphi, the University of California established a Study Centre for Classical Drama there in 1966. Forty students from Europe and America, interested in the theatre, were invited to spend six months in Delphi studying the modern Greek language and civilization against its classical background, and receiving

N

extensive training in Greek drama and literature under their own and visiting professors.

The inauguration of an International Theatre Festival is only part of the re-awakening of Delphi. Dionysos is acknowledged in the theatre, but there still remains Apollo, and the development of man's whole personality. The dreams of Sikelianos have not passed unobserved and in different parts of the world men have been considering his words, realizing the need for a revival of the 'Delphic Idea'.

The two great meeting-places of the ancient world were Olympia and Delphi. It is more than seventy years since the modern Olympic Games were founded and first held in Athens, under the patronage of the King of Greece. The founder of the modern Olympics was Baron Pierre de Coubertin, who considered that one reason for the glory of the Golden Age of Greece was the emphasis on physical culture. He hoped that the games would lead to a better understanding between diverse national groups gathered in fair competition. In the words of the closing speech of the president of the games there is a call to youth to 'display cheerfulness and concord so that the Olympic torch may be carried on with ever greater eagerness, courage and humanity for the good of humanity throughout the ages'. The modern Olympic Games, from a small beginning, spread in scope until they became an event of world-wide importance.

Sikelianos believed that Delphi played a far greater part in the creation of a Golden Age of Greece, than did Olympia. The Delphic Festival did not depend on physical prowess alone, but on competition for excellence in artistic and intellectual achievement as well, an aspect that was never very successfully adopted by the modern Olympics, although an attempt was made to include the arts. Under the influence of Delphi, a true pan-Hellenic unity was achieved. Even when the political concord, which should have followed the precepts of Apollo, was absent, the sharing of art and ideas produced a tremendous forward surge in the development of man's genius in the world of the spirit. Now, as in the past, there are great possibilities for the advancement of better international understanding through the arts. National boundaries have always seemed less rigid to the artist and the men of the theatre than to others.

In making its influence felt in the difficult task of trying to bring harmony among the forces which divide mankind, although deeply loved, Delphi was often the scene of discord, and even today its revival has occasionally led to disputes and arguments. Nevertheless it has been associated with the fondest dreams of men for a united world. The Council of Europe,[1] itself the scene of many disappointments and setbacks, in its attempts to form a parliament of Europe, has moved to restore Delphi to its place as cultural centre of Europe. The announcement of this decision read: 'Delphi according to the ancients was the cradle of civilisation, and its purpose was such as to maintain security and the stability of peace among various cultures, and the extension of the virtues to all civilised nations through the tightening of spiritual ties and cultural relations.' It was agreed that an International Centre should be built in Delphi, to be known as the 'Institute of International Ideas', for the exhibition of works of art and other cultural achievements of various European countries. At first it was planned to have a number of small buildings, each contributed by a member of the Council of Europe, following the example of the ancient treasuries of the sanctuary of Apollo, but it was finally decided to have a single centre with exhibition halls, conference rooms, a library and a theatre. It is intended that conferences and exhibitions should be held and that there should be music festivals, in addition to the drama festivals in the theatre of Delphi. The Greek Press reported that, 'Tourists going to Delphi will be able to visit the exhibitions, and will hear lectures by distinguished scholars on the theme of the European Idea and the way it has spread. It is indisputable that the establishment of the "Spiritual Centre" in Delphi will have the utmost importance in the projection of Greece into the civilised world of our century.'

To the matter-of-fact visitor, the exploitation of Delphi may seem to be a side-show to attract tourists. An isolated village in Greece does not really appear to have any significant connection with the serious business of world affairs or international relations. Greece undoubtedly needs more tourist traffic, but there will be many who will feel that Delphi has changed for the

[1] The Council of Europe was formed in 1949. Winston Churchill, an enthusiastic supporter of its aims, then said, 'The first step has been taken, and it is the first step that counts.'

worse. It is no longer the quiet village it was a few years ago.
Each year more tourists come, more souvenir shops and restaurants
are opened, and more hotels are being built, some with a
modern luxury which attempts to insulate the traveller from the
primitive powers that still exist in Delphi. In spite of the
increased prosperity, however, the Delphians still live very close
to their old way of life, which has changed very little for thousands
of years. The tourists bring the money, which is so desperately
needed, but the flocks of sheep and goats must be tended on the
high pastures, and the vines and olives harvested. The people of
Delphi are still sturdy mountain folk, as they were long ago when
they defied invading armies, or welcomed visitors bringing gifts,
and at the time of its greatest influence, over 2,000 years ago,
Delphi had far more hotels and sellers of tourist souvenirs than
it has now, or is likely to have in the near future.

To the Greek Tourist Organization, the publicity of a
Delphic Festival is, of course, an added impetus to encourage
people to visit Greece, and will succeed in expanding the much
needed tourist industry, but beneath the efforts of commercial
promotion lies a far deeper motive. The Greeks earnestly
believe in the validity of their efforts to re-animate their
ancient culture, the fruits of which are to be found, not only
in Greece, but throughout the world. There is a traditional
respect and even veneration of the remains of their past. In
Athens, when they were planning the Delphic Festival, I was
told quite seriously, 'It must be drama that we have in
Delphi; after all, it is a religious centre.'

The dream of a re-awakening 'Delphic Idea' may be a
romantic fancy and no more, but the visitor to Delphi cannot
but feel that there is indeed some ancient force still at work.
The legend said that Apollo came there and killed the Python
which guarded the powers of the Earth, and from the rotting
of the carcass 'germed and blossomed the strength of the god
of harmony, light and prophecy'.

It was a modern Greek poet and Nobel prize-winner, George
Seferis, who said: 'It is as if we have completed a full circle,
and we find ourselves, once again, faced with the anger of
natural forces without knowing how to control them. It is as
if we must have a new Pythia, and we have need of an Apollo,
if these names mean anything at all.'

Chronology: Delphi during the last 4,000 years

Before 2000 B.C.	Neolithic men use the pass over Parnassos.
2000–1700 B.C.	Bronze Age. Invasion by Achaeans. Kirra founded.
1700–1400	Krissos built. Mycenaean Age. Worship of Ge at Delphi.
1200–1100	Dorian invasion and settlement. Coming of Apollo.
1100–700	Geometric period.
750–700	The fame of Delphi spreads rapidly.
700–600	Age of colonization. Delphi established as the supreme authority on all colonization problems, and its influence spreads along the coast of the Mediterranean.
595	First Sacred War. Delphic lands extended to the sea. Conquest of Krissos.
590–550	Twelve treasuries built. The political influence of Delphi very great, and Greek states make use of its prestige for their own ends.
548	Temple burnt down and rebuilt.
480	Persians attack Delphi.
448	Second Sacred War. Decline in influence of Delphi.
373	Destruction of temple in earthquake. Rebuilding interrupted by
356	Third Sacred War.
338	Philip of Macedon conquers Greece.
279	Aetolians in power. Attack by Gauls. Delphi no longer of any political importance but remains religious and intellectual capital.
191	'Liberation' by the Romans. In spite of guarantees of autonomy to Delphi, it was often treated with little respect by the Romans, and the sanctuary was pillaged. The oracle became silent.
A.D. 48–122	Plutarch. Short but brilliant Renaissance of Delphi under emperors like Hadrian who revered the spirit of Greece.

185

148–180	Visit of Pausanias.
398	Proscription of Paganism. Destruction of temple. Byzantine Age begins. Delphi becomes 'Kastri'.
1676	Wheeler and Spon rediscover 'Delphes'.
1892	Archaeological excavations begin.
1927	First of the new Delphic Festivals, under Sikelianos.
1965	Building of Spiritual Centre of Council of Europe planned.
1966	Study Centre for Classical Drama inaugurated.
1967	First International Drama Festival planned.

Bibliography

Works consulted include the following:
Aeschylus, *Eumenides*. Translated by Gilbert Murray. London, 1925.
— *Prometheus Bound. Prometheus and Other Plays*. Translated by Philip Vellacott. London, 1961.
Annual Reports of the Committee on the American School of Classical Studies at Athens. Cambridge, Mass. Nos. 8, 9 and 10. 1889–91.
Amandry, Pierre, *La Mantique Apollienne à Delphes. Essai sur le fonctionnement de l'oracle*. Bibliothèque des Écoles Françaises d'Athènes et de Rome. Paris, 1950.
Bourguet, Emile, *Les Ruines de Delphes*. Paris, 1914.
Byron, Lord, *Childe Harold's Pilgrimage*, with notes. 1812.
Callimachus. Translated by A. W. Mair. London, 1921.
Cook, A. B., *Zeus*. Vol. II. A Study in Ancient Religion. Cambridge, 1925.
Diodorus Siculus, *World History*. Book XVI. Translated by Charles L. Sherman. London, 1952.
Dunkerley, Roderic, *Beyond the Gospels*. London, 1957.
Euripides, *Iphigenia in Tauris*. Translated by Gilbert Murray. London, 1910.
— *Bacchae*. Translated by Gilbert Murray. London, 1911.
— *Ion. Medea and Other Plays*. Translated by Philip Vellacott. London, 1954.
Farnell, L. R., *Cults of the Greek States*. Vol. IV. Oxford, 1900.
Flacelière, *Le Fonctionnement de l'Oracle de Delphes*. Ghent, 1938.
Fontenrose, Joseph, *Python*. California, 1959.
Fouilles de Delphes. École Française d'Athènes, 1927–52, particularly: *Topography and Architecture*. 1927; *Treasury of Kyrene*. 1952.
Frazer, Sir J. G., *Pausanias and other Greek Sketches*. London, 1900.
Glaspell, Susan, *The Road to the Temple*. London, 1928.
Graves, Robert, *Greek Myths*. London, 1958.
Gray, Thomas, *Progress of Poesy. Collected Poems*. Oxford, 1950.
Hamilton, Edith, *The Echo of Greece*. New York, 1957.
Harrison, Jane, *Prolegomena to the Study of Greek Religion*. Third Edition. Cambridge, 1922.
Hauptmann, Gerhart, *Griechischer Frühling*. Berlin, 1908.
Herodotus, *History*. Translated by Henry Cary. London, 1847.
Heschel, Abraham, *The Prophets*. New York, 1962.

Hesiod, Callimachus and Theognis. Translated by J. Banks. London, 1856.

Hesiod and Homeric Hymns. Translated by H. G. Evelyn-White. London, 1914.

Holland, Leicester B. *The Mantic Mechanism at Delphi*. *American Journal of Archaeology, XXXVII*. 1933.

Homer, *Odyssey*. Translated by E. V. Rieu. London, 1946.

Jannoray J., and van Effenterre, H., *Excavations at Krissa*. *Bulletin Hellénique, LXII*. 1938.

Jeans, Sir James, *The Mysterious Universe*. Cambridge, 1930.

— *Science and Music*. Cambridge, 1937.

Kakouri, Katerina, *Dionysiaka*. Athens, 1963.

Kerenyi, Carl, *The Gods of the Greeks*. London, 1951.

Lucan, *Pharsalia*. Translated by Robert Graves. London, 1956.

Misch, G., *A History of Autobiography in Antiquity*. Vol. II. Cambridge, 1951.

Messelière, P. de la Cost-, *Delphes*. Paris, 1943.

Nilsson, N. M. P., *A History of Greek Religion*. Translated by F. J. Fielden. Oxford, 1949.

Oppé, A. P., *Chasm*. *Journal of Hellenic Studies, XXIV*. 1904.

Ovid, *Metamorphoses*. Translated by Arthur Golding. 1567.

Pallotino, M., *The Etruscans*. London, 1955.

Parke, H. W., *A History of the Delphic Oracle*. Oxford, 1939.

Pausanias, *Description of Greece*. Translated by A. R. Shilleto. London, 1886.

Payne, Robert, *The Splendour of Greece*. London, 1961.

Pindar, *Odes*. Translated by E. M. Myers. London, 1892.

Plato, *The Last Days of Socrates*. Translated by Hugh Tredennick. London, 1955.

— *The Republic*. Translated by D. H. P. Lee. London, 1955.

Plutarch, *Parallel Lives*. Translated by Sir Thomas North. 1579.

— *Moralia*. Translated by C. W. King. London, 1903.

Radet, G., *Histoire de L'École Française d'Athènes*. Paris, 1901.

Rose, H. J., *Handbook of Greek Mythology*. London, 1928.

Seltman, Charles, *The Twelve Olympians*. London, 1952.

Sophocles, *The Theban Plays*. Translated by E. F. Watling. London, 1947.

— *Antigone*. Translated by R. Broughton. 1887.

Strabo, *Geography*. Translated by H. L. Jones. London, 1924.

Thucydides, *The Peloponnesian War*. Translated by Rex Warner. London, 1954.

Toynbee, Arnold, *Greek Historical Thought*. London, 1950.

Wellesz, E., *Byzantine Music and Hymnography*. Oxford, 1961.

Willets, R. E., *Cretan Cults and Festivals*. London, 1962.

Woodhouse, W. J., *Apollo. Encyclopaedia of Religion and Ethics*. 1908.

Index

189